FALL FOLIAGE

Fall Foliage

The Mystery, Science, and Folklore of Autumn Leaves

Charles W. G. Smith

Photographs by Frank Kaczmarek

FALCON GUIDE®

GUILFORD, CONNECTICUT
HELENA, MONTANA
AN IMPRINT OF THE GLOBE PEQUOT PRESS

Falcon and FalconGuide are registered trademarks of The Globe Pequot Press.

Maps © The Globe Pequot Press
Text design: Nancy Freeborn

Library of Congress Cataloging-in-Publication Data
Smith, Charles W. G.
    Fall foliage: the mystery, science, and folklore of autumn leaves/Charles W. G. Smith—1st ed.
      p. cm.
    ISBN 0-7627-2788-8
      1. Leaves—Folklore. 2. Fall foliage—Folklore. 3. Autumn—Folklore. I. Title.
    GR790.L33S65 2003
    398'.368–dc21

                                                                2003047141

Manufactured in the United States of America
First Edition/First Printing

To buy books in quantity for corporate use
or incentives, call **(800) 962–0973, ext. 4551,**
or e-mail **premiums@GlobePequot.com.**

To my loving wife Susan,
whose joy, compassion, and spirit bring so much happiness to my life.
Thank you for our "perfect bond of union."

(Colossians 3:14)

Contents

Introduction

A Celebration of Color

Fall foliage in North America is so strikingly beautiful that it creates wonderful memories that last a lifetime. There's the joy of jumping into big piles of freshly raked fallen leaves. Kids playing beneath maple trees, trying to catch each twirling crimson leaf as it falls. The thrill of walking through a shower of sunny yellow leaves blown from the trees by a reckless breath of wind. A stroll down a country lane on a brisk autumn day, a quilt of warm-colored leaves rustling with each step. And the breathtaking view from a height of land that overlooks rolling hills where brilliant reds, oranges, and yellows flow on until they fade on the distant horizon like a Monet.

A Unique Experience

Fall foliage across the continent is such a spectacular and memorable experience because it is as rare as it is wonderful. Colorful fall foliage is an uncommon occurrence on Earth that requires the coinciding of several factors, such as moisture, day length, latitude, plant species, temperature, and even the mineral content of the soil. So many variables must fall into place for a region to produce striking fall foliage that these autumn displays are limited to just three regions of the world: portions of eastern Asia, including China and Japan; a small area of central South America; and a large portion of North America. Even these privileged areas are not equal in the intensity, scale, and length of season. Although each area has unique character and splendor, the brilliant forests in North America have color and presence so intense that they captivate the senses.

Experiences to Treasure

If you envision the most spectacular scenes of fall foliage as hidden treasure, then imagine this book as a treasure map. Like all good treasure hunts, you need to know a little about the prize you're seeking, such as where it is and how to get there. This book provides all of that and more. The first part, "A Field Guide," tells you all about the different trees and shrubs that light up the forest each fall. The second part, "Bright Spots," details where to go to enjoy this incredible annual delight as well as various ways to get there—by foot, car, train, or boat. Scattered throughout the book are stories and pictures that will help you discover and celebrate the splendor of fall foliage in America. So venture forth to enjoy the treasure that is renewed every year, and rediscover the beauty over and over again!

The Science of Fall Foliage

The largest and oldest living things on Earth are trees. The largest known tree is a giant sequoia about 250 feet tall with a trunk estimated to weigh nearly three million pounds. A bristlecone pine that is now nearly 4,800 years old was growing in the mountains of California centuries before Moses wrote the first books of the Bible. Although there are tens of thousands of species of trees, these remarkable plants all have similar features that allow them to dominate and beautify the landscape.

Parts of a Tree

Crown. The leaves and branches are collectively called the crown. The green leaves produce food for the plant through a process called photosynthesis, which uses sunlight, carbon dioxide, and water to make sugars. The crown also filters pollution from the air, slows the wind, provides shelter for wildlife, and provides shade.

Roots. Trees have two types of roots: thin feeder roots and stronger anchor roots. The tiny feeder roots absorb moisture and nutrients, whereas the larger anchor roots store food and hold the tree in the soil. Some trees, like oaks, have anchoring roots called taproots that grow deep into the ground. All trees have lateral roots—anchoring roots that grow out from the tree, most of them less than 2 feet below ground.

Trunk. The trunk supports the branches and canopy of leaves. It also is filled with an intricate plumbing system of tubes, some bringing water and nutrients to the leaves from the roots and others carrying food from the leaves to the roots.

Wood. The wood of trees is made of cells called xylem *(ZY-lem)*. These tubular cells carry water and nutrients from the roots to the leaves and provide support for the upper portions of the tree.

Cambium. This thin layer of cells is the heart of the tree, producing both wood (xylem) and inner bark (phloem [*FLO-em*]). The cambium is what makes the tree grow in diameter every year.

Inner bark is made of tubular cells called phloem that carry the sugary sap made in the leaves down the stem to the roots for storage.

Bark. The bark that covers the tree is made of old phloem cells that no longer serve as a piping system but now protect the tree from the elements, disease, and pests.

Where Does Fall Color Come From?

The beauty of a landscape burning with fall color can be so awe inspiring that this simple but thought-provoking question is never asked. After all, the leaves on the trees have been green for months. Why does the green suddenly vanish, and where do the other colors mysteriously come from?

One of the principal jobs of a leaf is to act as a solar collector, gathering in sunlight to use in photosynthesis. Photosynthesis uses carbon dioxide, water, and sunlight in the presence of specific chemicals called pigments to produce sugars that the plant needs for food. There are three primary pigments in a leaf: chlorophyll, carotene, and anthocyanin.

- *Chlorophyll* is the chemical that makes leaves look green. It also does most of the work of turning sunlight into sweet glucose. Interestingly, chlorophyll breaks down in the presence of sunlight and has to be continually replaced during the growing season by the plant. Yet the plant can only manufacture chlorophyll when the weather is warm and there is enough daylight.

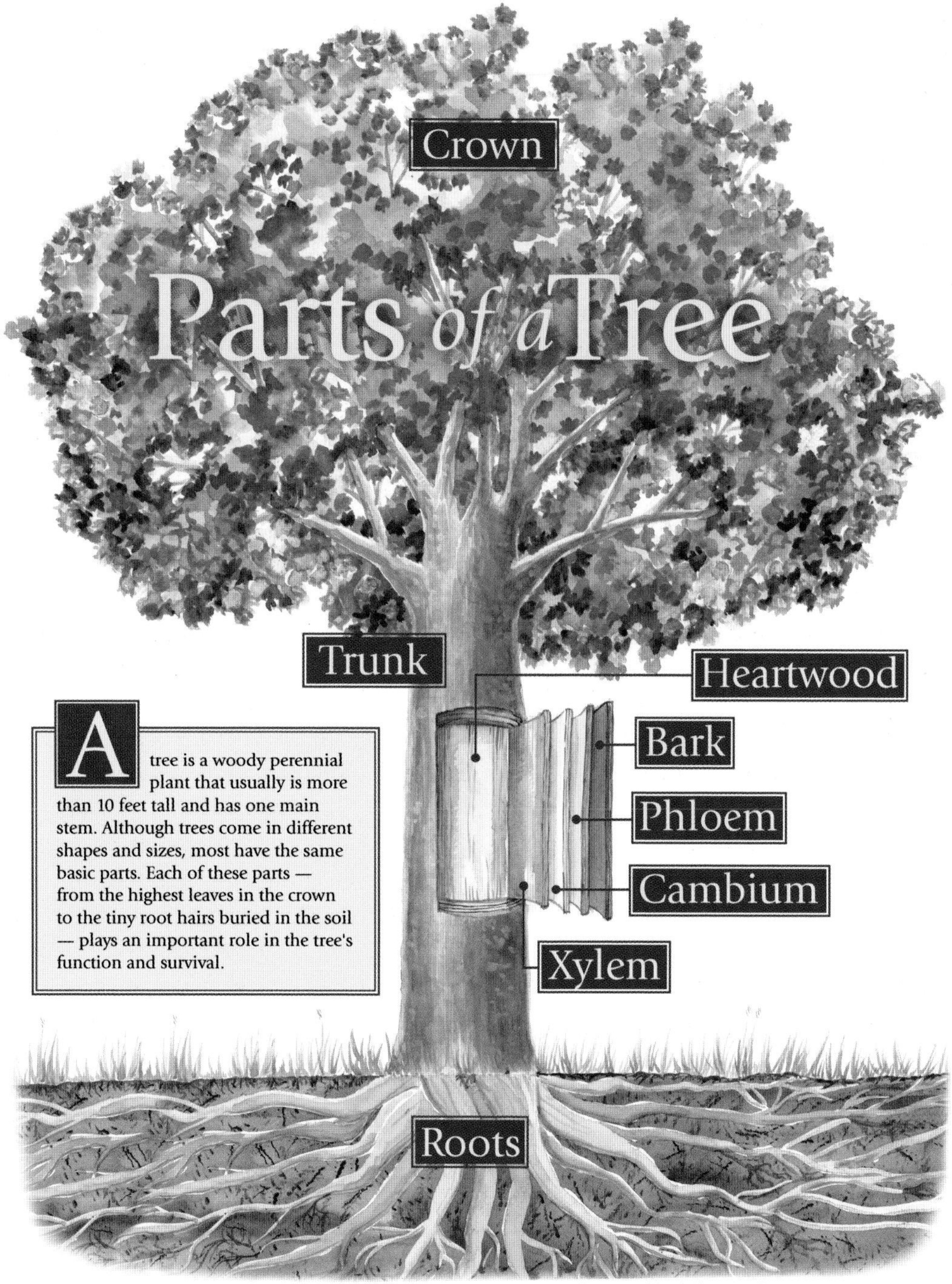

Crown
Parts of a Tree
Trunk
Heartwood
Bark
Phloem
Cambium
Xylem
Roots
A tree is a woody perennial plant that usually is more than 10 feet tall and has one main stem. Although trees come in different shapes and sizes, most have the same basic parts. Each of these parts — from the highest leaves in the crown to the tiny root hairs buried in the soil — plays an important role in the tree's function and survival.

Courtesy North Carolina Forestry Association

- *Carotenes* are found in the same part of the leaf as chlorophyll. These yellow, red, or brown pigments help protect chlorophyll from sunlight—for a little while, at least—and aid in photosynthesis. The bright yellow color of daffodils and buttercups and the red of ripe tomatoes are due to the presence of carotenes.
- *Anthocyanins* are pigments that come in red, purple, blue, and other complementary shades, such as scarlet. They make cherries red, grapes purple, and morning-glorys blue. During the growing season the amount of anthocyanin in leaves is low, and it doesn't have an impact on the color of the leaf.

Weather Conditions and Leaf Color

Warm weather, especially warm nights, allows the tree to keep sending sugars from the leaves to the roots. If enough sugar is removed from the foliage, the resulting leaf color will be muted. Cold nights inhibit transport of sugar and result in much brighter coloration. A summer of cloudy, rainy weather—a common pattern in the southern Appalachian Mountains—inhibits the manufacture of sugars. Thus the resulting autumn color, especially shades of orange and red, is pale and short-lived.

Changing Seasons, Changing Colors

How many psychiatrists does it take to change a leaf? Only one, but the leaf has to really want to change.

Bad jokes aside, what does make a leaf that has been green for months suddenly "want" to change color? Leaves turn color and drop in response to a host of different factors working in concert. The chief factor, however, is the rapidly diminishing length of daylight. This change in the balance of day and night initiates a cascade of biochemical changes in the leaf.

As the weather cools, the creation of chlorophyll stops. The last chlorophyll in the leaves degrades, and the green color of the leaf disappears. In preparation for winter the plant begins to sever the leaf from the twig. As this progresses, the warm days and cool nights of late summer and early fall stimulate the production of sugars and anthocyanins in the leaf. As the leaf prepares to fall, the narrowing veins trap sugars and pigments in the leaf blade, spurring the creation of peak color.

Peak Splendor

All these factors contribute to the eventual color of the leaf. Although the green of the chlorophyll is gone, the decomposition products of the degraded chlorophyll molecules turn leaves a rich gold hue. Carotenes once overlain by the chlorophyll radiate bright yellow shades. When anthocyanins are abundant, they override other pigments and turn the leaf every shade of red.

The final polish of brilliance comes through the interactions of factors including soil moisture, day and night temperatures, amount and timing of

What Makes Leaves Turn Yellow?

If the leaves of a tree don't hold much glucose and don't contain lots of natural waste material, the foliage just reflects the colors of the pigments left behind after the chlorophyll is gone. These trees, including quaking aspen and tamarack, display a pure, clear yellow color that can seem as bright as sunlight.

Some of the things plants expend energy on always use more than they produce. For example, creating seeds requires energy, but the seeds never contribute energy back. They are produced to perpetuate the species, not enrich the parent plant. Leaves, however, are different. Nearly all the photosynthetic activity—the process that converts the sun's energy to food—happens in the leaves of the plant. In business terms, the leaves are where the profit is made. They are the cornerstone of the whole company; lose them and you go bankrupt. If they are so important, why do plants lose their leaves every fall?

sunlight and rain, as well as latitude and plant heredity. Warm nights when the leaves are turning can dull the colors. Drought can hasten color change and leaf drop, and a warm wet summer can delay it for weeks. The exact recipe for what makes the best fall foliage color can be debated forever—because no one really knows how everything fits together. But the splendid and unique beauty every fall is indisputable.

Why Do Leaves Fall?

Trees and shrubs are excellent economists that use energy as their currency rather than money. For a business to make a profit, it has to earn more money than it spends. For a plant to survive, it must make more food (energy) than it expends. Just as a business spends money on numerous things, a plant uses energy to accomplish tasks ranging from growing and flowering to fruit and seed formation.

What Makes Leaves Turn Red?

Many factors determine the eventual color a leaf will turn after its chlorophyll disappears. Photosynthesis creates glucose within the leaf. Most of the glucose is then moved out of the leaf to other parts of the plant. If the glucose becomes trapped in the leaf as the tree prepares to drop its leaves in fall, the leaves will turn orange, scarlet, or red. As a general rule, the more glucose in the leaf, the brighter the color.

Trees with bright red foliage include sugar maple, sourwood, and staghorn sumac.

Natural systems often exhibit wisdom that human ones do not. Leaves of deciduous species are constructed to be solar collectors as well as vents for moisture and gas exchange. To do these tasks most efficiently, the leaf should be paper-thin and made of plant cells that are specifically designed to be extremely efficient at performing their tasks. The trade-off is that the same things that make the leaves so efficient also make them vulnerable to certain environmental conditions, especially cold.

On a below-zero morning in winter, the trees you see in the forest are frozen solid. They are brittle, creating the eerie creak and crack in the wind. But winter cold doesn't kill them—although below-zero temperatures in spring would. As cold settles over the countryside, the water inside the cells is funneled out

of them, where it freezes harmlessly in intercellular empty spaces. If cold comes too quickly and the water isn't moved out in time, the water freezes within the cells. The types of cells and the thin nature of leaves make them very sensitive to freezing. Leaves that freeze and die on the tree remain clinging to the branches, providing an avenue for infection and pest infestation. The way to solve all these problems is for the leaves to drop before the real cold of winter sets in.

Leaf fall is a wonderfully designed process, succinct in its simplicity and elegant in arrangement. Between the leaf stem (petiole) and the branch of every leaf is a region of specialized cells called the separation layer. As the growing season ends, the pectin within the walls of these cells is dissolved by enzymes. The cells then shrink, and the petiole separates from the branch. All that keeps the leaf attached now is a thin connection of vascular tissue in the center of the petiole. Sunny warm days slowly dry up the petiole, and the connection between leaf and tree becomes as ephemeral as spider silk. The next falling raindrop or passing breeze knocks the leaf free, and it sails away in a graceful free fall to the ground. Where the leaf once was is a small bud that, come spring, will be transformed into next year's leaves.

How to Use This Book

Fall Foliage is an easy-to-use guide to help you find the best fall color in North America. The book is divided into two sections. The first part describes the most popular and attractive fall foliage trees and shrubs in North America. The second part tours the country's most featured foliage locations, presenting driving tours through the countryside and hikes through the woods. Either way, you will enjoy autumn's splendor.

The first part, "A Field Guide," helps you recognize the most popular and colorful plants of fall by focusing first on what they look like in that season. At the top of the page each plant is identified by its common name, its scientific name, and the name of the plant family to which it belongs. A general description of the plant is followed by a description of its fall appearance. Then you'll read where the plant can be found—its favorite terrain, such as wetlands or ridges, and what trees and shrubs it grows with. Tree Facts and Shrub Stuff provide interesting information about the plant. A range map depicts where in the country the plant can be found. Some plants have a small native range—or no native range—but their popularity as landscape trees has expanded their range well beyond their native area.

The second part of the book, "Bright Spots," is a tour of the country's most renowned foliage destinations. This section divides the best foliage areas in the nation into geographic regions, such as New England or the Rocky Mountains, where the forests, landscape, and timing of peak foliage are similar. You'll also find descriptions of driving tours and hikes through picturesque places.

A Field Guide

Trees of the Forest and Countryside

Ash | *Fraxinus* spp.

There are many North American species of ash. The two most common and widely distributed are white ash and green ash. White ash grows about 80 feet tall, with green ash slightly shorter. The leaves are arranged in rows of five to nine leaflets growing on either side of a central leaf stem. The rough diamond pattern bark is pewter gray and particularly attractive.

Ash in Fall

White and green ash can be often distinguished from other trees and from each other by the color of their fall foliage. The leaves of white ash turn dull purple to reddish violet, whereas those of green ash become yellow. The leaves of ash trees turn early in the foliage season and do not hold well, seemingly impatient to leave the branch for their short dance on the wind.

Where to Find Ash

Ash trees are found in many varied forest types throughout most of eastern North America. The trees can be locally abundant, often growing with maples, oaks, cherry, and pine in habitats ranging from the edges of fields to mature forest and from valley to ridge crest. Both trees are also used in landscaping and are common in parks, backyards, and botanical gardens.

Tree Facts

The United States National Champion white ash lives in the front yard of Montebello's Italian Restaurant off Route 9W in Palisades, New York. This tree has a trunk circumference of more than 25 feet and stands 95 feet tall, with a canopy more than 80 feet across.

Aspens | *Populus* spp.

Aspens are hardy and adaptable, growing from Maryland to Labrador and Alaska to Mexico. Aspen bark is smooth and greenish white, with young trees rivaling birches in their attractiveness. Older trees grow about 60 feet tall but occasionally reach 100 feet. The round leaves dangle from the branches by flattened leaf stems, making the foliage quiver when stirred by the breeze.

Aspens in Fall

In fall the silvery green foliage is soaked in shades of canary yellow and molten gold. When the leaves are backlit against a blue autumn sky, they appear nearly translucent and glow with color. In some of the mountain canyons of the Rockies, groves of aspens are so brilliant they seem to shine with their own light. Most aspens are yellow, but the leaves of some turn sunset orange. Aspens grow in groves, often in pure stands that amplify the color of the foliage.

Where to Find Aspens

Aspens grow on mountain slopes and in abandoned fields, clear-cuts, burned areas, and other disturbed places. They are the principal trees in the fall displays of many western states, where they put on a spectacular show. In western areas aspens seek out more sheltered places such as inside canyons, alongside creeks, and on lee slopes.

Tree Facts

Perhaps the largest aspen tree grows in Kootenai National Forest in Troy, Montana. This tree has a circumference of 8 feet and stands 144 feet tall. The most massive aspen relative is the eastern cottonwood, with the largest specimen probably growing in Balmville, New York. This huge tree is 83 feet tall with a circumference of 25 feet.

Beech | *Fagus grandifolia*

Beech trees are attractive hardwoods with wide-spreading branches and thin, very smooth icy gray bark. The leaves are oblong and coarsely toothed. In fall small edible nuts encased in a bristly husk appear on the branches.

Beech Trees in Fall

The foliage of beeches generally turns color later than most other trees. The color seeps over the leaf like a slowly rising tide, turning the foliage from green to yellow with green along the veins, then solid yellow-bronze. As the days go on, the color deepens to tarnished bronze, then solidifies into an even brown. The leaves remain on the tree through winter until the expanding leaf buds release their grip.

Where to Find Beech Trees

Beech trees are often found in pure stands of mixed age, with individuals ranging from young to very old. Beech groves are very attractive places; a stroll through these trees makes you feel as if you're walking through Camelot. Beeches also grow among a number of other trees, including sugar maples, oaks, cherry, pine, birch, eastern hemlock, ash, and hickory. In warmer climates they grow with sweetgum, ash, oaks, pine, and southern magnolia. They are popular landscaping trees, with large specimens commonly found in many parks, backyards, and botanical gardens.

BEECH FAMILY

Tree Facts

The largest North American beech is generally considered to be in Harwood, Maryland. This tree is 115 feet tall, with a canopy stretching 138 feet and a trunk circumference of more than 23 feet.

Birches | *Betula* spp.

Birches are beautiful trees with attractive, often peeling bark and warm fall leaf colors. The most common species are paper birch, black birch, yellow birch, and river birch. All have a similar shape, form, and height, with strong trunks and a full crown of branches reaching more than 80 feet tall.

Birches in Fall

Birches often grow in large stands that glow with intense color in fall. River birch has foliage of burnished bronze, whereas the leaves of black, yellow, and paper birches turn shades of lemon and saffron. Walking beneath a stand of birches at peak color is exhilarating. The thin-textured foliage diffuses the light and drenches the woods with a golden glow even on cloudy days.

Where to Find Birches

Paper birch is a hardy tree found across much of northern North America. It prefers cool mountainsides, ravines, and shores of streams and lakes. Also look for paper birch in old fields, logged areas, burned-over forest, or other disturbed places.

Yellow and black birches grow from northeastern Canada through much of the Appalachians and west to the northern Mississippi Valley. The trees grow in moist uplands along with aspen, pine, cherry, maple, and ash. River birch thrives along rivers and streams from southern New England to Iowa and south to the Gulf Coast.

Tree Facts

The sap of the sweet birch contains large amounts of methyl salicylate, better known as oil of wintergreen. It is used in small amounts to flavor and scent such popular products as soda and liniment. Products with high concentrations of methyl salicylate, as in birch essential oil, can be toxic and should be used with caution.

Elms | *Ulmus* spp.

Elms have rough, oblong leaves lined with sawlike teeth. The bark is coarse, furrowed, and grayish. The trees grow from about 60 to more than 120 feet tall, depending on species. American elm is the most attractive; its distinctively handsome vase-shaped form makes it easy to identify even from far away. Slippery elm is similar but does not have as attractive a shape.

Elms in Fall

Elm foliage turns a warm russet yellow in fall, with many of the leaves retaining streaks and splotches of green amid the gold. American elms are especially handsome, the stately vase shape and dusky golden foliage combining to give the tree the distinguished look of a valued antique.

Where to Find Elms

Slippery, rock, and other forest elms prefer the wet soils of swamps and poorly drained wooded areas. They commonly grow with pines, willow, and ash. American elms grow almost anywhere but are most handsome in open areas such as windrows, fields, and pastures. American elm grows throughout most of North America east of the Rockies. Rock elm is a tree of the Midwest, and slippery elm thrives in the eastern forests.

Tree Facts

Dutch elm disease is a fungus that came to Europe from Asia during World War I and virtually wiped out European elms. The disease was discovered in 1930 in Ohio and has since decimated elms across North America. Research has produced resistant trees that can now be purchased in nurseries and garden centers.

The largest known American elm grows between two cornfields in Buckley, Michigan. This tree, perhaps as old as 400 years, is more than 110 feet tall.

Hickories | *Carya* spp.

Hickories are handsome and resilient trees with sturdy trunks and a scaffold of strong branches. The leaves are composed of about seven large leaflets arranged along a central stem. The foliage has a sweet and pungent odor when bruised, a quality best appreciated while lying in a pile of freshly raked leaves. Hickories grow to 100 feet tall and produce a hard-shelled, edible nut encased in a husk.

Hickories in Fall

Hickory trees have foliage that runs from tarnished bronze in shagbark hickory to tranquil yellow in mockernut. The colors are warm and comfortable like a candle burning in a window at dusk. Many hickory species grow on droughty soils, and in dry years the leaves often become scorched at the margins, adding a cast of brown to the overall effect.

Where to Find Hickories

Nearly all hickories prefer deep soils and well-drained hillsides, bluffs, and uplands throughout eastern North America from central New England west to the edge of the Great Plains and south to the Gulf and Atlantic Coasts. They are most often solitary or peppered throughout hardwood forests in company with oaks, beech, and maple.

Tree Facts

The name *hickory* probably derives from several similar Algonquian words and phrases that described the nut and its uses by Native Americans. The deep roots of hickories absorb many minerals from deep within the subsoil and bring these nutrients to the leaves. When the leaves drop, they make the topsoil more fertile by adding important minerals.

Maple, Red | *Acer rubrum*

Red maple is a beautifully ornamental tree with a spreading canopy of green leaves above a trunk with blackish gray bark. In the forest it grows straight and tall, whereas in open fields it has a thicker trunk and larger crown of leaves. Red maple can be found growing in many different environments, from swamps to mountaintops.

Red Maple in Fall

Red maples produce colors as bright as neon. In fall the foliage changes from green to an incredible number of shades, tones, and hues of red. As the foliage reaches its peak, the tree looks as hot as glowing embers in the fireplace. The foliage turns early in the season and often lasts for weeks.

Where to Find Red Maple

Red maples grow from southern Canada south to the Gulf Coast. The trees can adapt to flooded conditions, forming "red maple swamps"—nearly pure stands of stunted trees that turn beautiful colors very early in the season. Red maples prefer the banks of streams and shores of lakes and ponds as well as moist woodlands, where they can reach 100 feet tall. They grow with arborvitae, ash, hornbeam, and tamarack. The leaves turn earlier than other trees and can be easily spotted amid the surrounding green forest.

MAPLE FAMILY

Tree Facts

The many species of maple trees may look very similar, but the wood they yield is very different. Maple wood is categorized as either hard or soft. Hard maple is used for high-quality furniture and comes from sugar and black maples. Soft maple is a slightly lesser grade and comes from box elder, red maple, and silver maple.

Maple, Sugar | *Acer saccharum*

The sugar maple is a majestic tree with a broad spreading crown and strong scaffold of upright branches. The lead-gray bark is often hidden behind the dense canopy of medium green leaves. In the kaleidoscopically beautiful and varied world of fall foliage, the burning, molten colors of the sugar maple are the standard by which all other trees are measured. Sugar maples can be distinguished from other maples by the U-shape at the base of the leaf lobes; other maples sport a V-shape.

Sugar Maple in Fall

The sugar maple is the signature tree of fall, with foliage that changes from medium green into a polychromatic swirl of warm sunset colors—from clear yellow to oriole orange, and from hot crimson to aged burgundy. Some trees can be one solid shade, whereas others sport sprays of different colors. Sugar maples retain their beauty for a long time and only reluctantly drop their leaves after many weeks.

Where to Find Sugar Maple

The sugar maple is common throughout eastern North America, from southern Canada to the southern Appalachians. It frequently grows with ash, oaks, birch, cherry, and other hardwoods but can also be found in nearly pure stands. Everywhere the sugar maple is found, it is esteemed and admired. Traditionally the place to find the most vibrant trees is New England and the surrounding states and provinces.

Tree Facts

In addition to its beauty, the sugar maple is the most valuable hardwood tree in America for its top-grade lumber and sweet maple sugar. The largest known sugar maple is 65 feet tall with a circumference of nearly 23 feet. It grows in Kitzmiller, Maryland.

Oak, Red (Red Oak, Black Oak, Scarlet Oak, Texas Oak, Pin Oak, Turkey Oak) | *Quercus* spp.

There are three groups of oaks—red oaks, white oaks, and live or ever-green oaks. The red oak group, more than the others, contains many trees with outstanding fall foliage. The leaves of red oaks look like the proverbial oak leaves, with a thin hair at the tip of each lobe. Red oaks have dark, nearly black bark and range from dwarf mountaintop species to trees more than 100 feet tall.

Red Oaks in Fall

The leaves of red oaks come in shades of blackish burgundy to scarlet. Their foliage display has an opaque quality that is very different from the light, translucent character of trees such as birch. Oak leaves eventually turn brown and linger on the tree well into winter.

Where to Find Red Oaks

Oaks require bright, sunny places with deep soil that is not too dry or too wet.

- Turkey oak *(Q. laevis)* is a shrubby tree that grows in tangled thickets in the sandy soils along the Atlantic Coast. The leaves are shaped somewhat like a turkey's foot and turn rich red in fall.
- Northern red oak *(Q. rubra)* is one of the largest oaks and ranges from the Midwest to New England. The fall color varies from scorched burgundy to hot scarlet.
- Shumard's oak *(Q. shumardii)* is a stately tree reaching 100 feet tall and looks very similar to northern red oak. It is the predominant oak in much of the lower Mississippi Valley. The leaves turn early in the season and have a polished blackish red color.
- The lowest branches of pin oak *(Q. palustris)* angle down toward the ground, making identification pretty easy. The foliage varies from scarlet to brownish red in fall. Pin oak is the most common oak in nurseries and is widespread in parks, along highway medians, and in yards and gardens.

Tree Facts

Quercus, the scientific name for oak, probably derives from the Celtic language and means "fine tree." The wood of this fine tree brings on allergic reactions in some people, producing skin rashes, sinus problems, and asthma.

Oak, White | *Quercus alba*

The white oak is a symbol of permanence, often growing for centuries. The gray-barked trunk is stout, with many strong branches forming a symmetrical spreading crown up to 80 feet tall and 100 feet wide. The leaves, marked with shallow lobes and rounded tips, are pink in spring and turn dark glossy green as they expand. The fruit is an acorn embraced in a scaly cap.

White Oak in Fall

In fall the medium green leaves turn subdued shades of purple-red that have a strong, deep quality unlike most other trees. The white oak is a patient tree and takes its time changing color in fall. The leaves reluctantly lose their green gloss days or weeks after other trees and cling to their foliage longer than many.

Where to Find White Oak

The white oak is a tree of the eastern United States, from Maine south to near the Gulf Coast. It's often seen in agricultural fields or pastures, providing shade for cows and scenery for us. White oaks thrive in deep, well-drained soils in company with hickories, red oaks, beech, and tulip trees. Farther south they grow with sweetgum, magnolia, and pecan.

Tree Facts

The white oak is a valuable timber tree, its durable wood used for everything from railroad ties to fine furniture. Oak was also used in making ships. Travel to places like Cape Cod and you'll often see the oak skeletons of old shipwrecks poking through the sand.

Sassafras | *Sassafras albidum*

The mitten-shaped leaves of sassafras make this one of the most recognizable trees. The hand-sized foliage suspended from the branches resembles dozens of mittens hanging on a fireplace hearth. The leaves can also be oval or three-lobed like a dinosaur footprint. The trees often reach 60 feet tall, with reddish brown, deeply furrowed bark. All parts of sassafras are intensely aromatic, with a warm spicy fragrance.

Caution: Safrole is a carcinogenic compound naturally found in sassafras. *Before purchasing any sassafras product, make sure it is safrole-free.*

Sassafras in Fall

Sassafras leaves come in a wide range of colors, from yellow to orange, red, and greenish purple. The most common colors are clear yellow or a warm crimson-orange.

Where to Find Sassafras

Sassafras likes to grow at the edges of abandoned fields, clearings, road cuts, hiking trails, or in the understory of open woods throughout eastern North America. Trees are sometimes solitary but more commonly found in small groves. In most of its range, sassafras can be found growing near pawpaw, flowering dogwood, sweetgum, and persimmon trees. At the northern edge of its range, companions include red oak and hornbeam.

LAUREL FAMILY

Tree Facts

The name *sassafras* probably derives from a mix of Native American, Spanish, and possibly French. It may have originally meant "breaker of stones," in reference to one of its medicinal uses in relief of kidney stones. In the early 1600s sassafras became the rage in Europe; tons of it was harvested and shipped there for a variety of uses from teas to soap.

Sourwood (Lily-of-the-Valley Tree)
Oxydendrum arboreum

Sourwood is esteemed for its beauty from spring through fall. This small, roughly pyramidal tree reaches about 60 feet tall but is usually smaller. The lance-shaped leaves are 4 to 8 inches long, dark green with a lustrous shine. In summer the tree is covered with white, bell-shaped flowers that are like a dinner bell for honeybees.

Sourwood in Fall

Few trees are in the same league as sourwood for fall color. In fall the deep green foliage metamorphoses to intense scarlet, with undertones of yellow and burgundy. The foliage defines the hundreds of long, very slender yellowish fruit capsules that decorate the tree. The beauty of the display is magnified by its endurance—sourwood leaves hold their color and hang on to the branches until late in the season.

Where to Find Sourwood

Sourwood is native from the southern Appalachians to the Atlantic Coast. In its range it is most common on slopes and ridges below 3,500 feet in elevation. The tree needs well-drained, sandy soils and often grows with oaks, sweetgum, hickory, buckeye, sugar maple, and pine. Its multiseason beauty makes it a popular tree in parks and yards within and beyond its natural range. When planted as an ornamental, sourwood prefers a sunny location protected from the wind.

HEATH FAMILY

Tree Facts

Sourwood gets its name from the acid taste of the leaves and twigs, which are used traditionally as a tonic. The genus Oxydendrum consists of only one species, sourwood, and is found only in America.

Sweetgum | *Liquidambar styraciflua*

The sweetgum tree reaches about 100 feet in height and about 3 feet in diameter, with corky gray bark and dark green maple- or star-shaped leaves. The trees, especially young trees, are beautifully symmetrical, with an upright, narrowly conical habit. Old trees seem massive and unmovable, with mighty trunks and towering canopies. The unique leaves, in the shape of a five-pointed star, make this tree a cinch to identify.

Sweetgum in Fall

Of the tree's many excellent qualities, fall color is perhaps the best. The leaves can range from yellow to orange, red, and purple, providing an eclectic riot of shades. Leaves on some trees can be nearly all one color—say, red or orange—whereas other trees are sporting a mix of wildly contrasting colors.

Where to Find Sweetgum

At the northern portion of its range, sweetgum trees can be found scattered throughout forests of oak, hickory, and some pines. Farther south where sweetgum trees are more abundant, they grow with many types of pines as well as oaks, sourwood, and cypress. They are common landscape plants in yards and parks, where they are planted for their fall color.

Tree Facts

The scientific name for sweetgum, *Liquidambar,* describes the golden resin produced by the tree: As you might expect, it means "liquid amber." The common name also refers to the resin, which has a sweet taste and sticky, gummy quality. The fruit of sweetgum trees is a small round capsule called a gumball.

Tamarack | *Larix laricina*

Tamarack trees are conifers like pines and spruces that, unlike their relatives, lose all their needles each fall in a wonderful blaze of color. Tamarack needles appear each spring in whorled bundles at the end of the twigs. In fall the needles turn a clear, uniform yellow and then drop to the ground. The cones of the tamarack are small and resemble those of the eastern hemlock. The trees grow in groves and have a symmetrical, conical shape similar to spruces.

Tamarack in Fall

Tamarack trees are beautifully symmetrical spires of soft yellow and gold that get their color from the seemingly infinite number of slender needles covering the rough-barked branches. When a grove of tamarack is viewed from a distance, each tree seems to melt into the next, creating a warm golden mass that intoxicates the senses.

Where to Find Tamarack

Tamarack trees most often grow in pure stands, preferring wet sodden places such as marshes and other wetlands where few other trees grow. They are easy to spot in fall when their golden color gives them away. The tamarack is among the hardiest of trees, surviving across Canada, even far above the Arctic Circle. Its southern limit is the southern Great Lakes east to New Jersey.

PINE FAMILY

Tree Facts

The largest known tamarack doesn't grow in the chilly northland but in Coventry, Connecticut. The tree is 62 feet tall with a trunk circumference of more than 12 feet. The name tamarack is derived from a Native American word meaning "wood for snowshoes."

Tulip Tree | *Liriodendron tulipifera*

The tulip tree can be enormous, historically reaching almost 200 feet tall. The massive trunk is as straight as an arrow, carrying a canopy of leaves high overhead. The large leaves have a unique shape, squared off at the tip with two wing-shaped lobes at the end, making the entire leaf look a little like a poorly designed mitten. The cup-shaped flowers are borne in spring on the uppermost branches and are colored orange and green.

Tulip Tree in Fall

In fall the leaves of the tulip tree turn from medium green to a metallic gold. The foliage display is not a uniform color. The leaves have a dominant shade of dark brass, with flecks of brighter gold sprayed throughout the canopy. In peak color the tree is striking, though many tulip trees are so tall they are best viewed from the base of the tree or from a distance.

Where to Find Tulip Tree

Tulip trees grow across eastern North America, where they appear as solitary trees in mixed forests with ash, maple, and eastern hemlock. They can be found scattered through fertile bottomlands along streams and rivers and on well-drained hillsides. Tulip trees, especially large specimens, are also found in parks and nature preserves.

Tree Facts

The name *tulip tree* comes from the tulip-shaped, upright green and orange flowers that appear in the topmost branches in early summer. The largest known tulip tree, also called yellow poplar, is in Bedford, Virginia. It stands 111 feet tall with a circumference of more than 30 feet.

Tupelo, Black (Sour Gum) | *Nyssa sylvatica*

Tupelo trees have shiny, leathery green leaves about 4 inches long that are clustered near the ends of the branches. The trees are conical in shape, growing about 80 feet tall and 3 feet in diameter. Smaller trees have a layered branching pattern that is very attractive. In spring the leafy canopies are alive with buzzing bees that use the nectar from the inconspicuous flowers to make honey. Black tupelo grows in the upland forests.

Tupelo in Fall

In fall the glossy leaves of tupelo trees turn deep crimson before gracefully aging to a polished mahogany red. The foliage color is deep, and the shiny leaves and rich tones make this a tree that will catch and hold on to your attention.

Where to Find Tupelo

Black tupelo is hardier than swamp tupelo and can be found throughout most of the eastern United States. It thrives in forests near streams and rivers where the soils are sandy. It can also be found in upland woods with oaks, hickories, and other hardwoods, as well as many types of pines. Swamp tupelo likes the heavy muck or clay soils of southern swamps and can often be found growing with bald cypress.

TUPELO FAMILY

Tree Facts

The word *tupelo* is derived from the Creek language and means "tree of the swamp." Swamp tupelo, a variety of black tupelo, is one of the few trees that grow in water. It is often found growing in southern swamps with bald cypress.

Shrubs, Small Trees, and Vines

Blueberries/Huckleberries | *Vaccinium* spp.

Blueberries are shrubs growing from less than 1 foot tall to more than 10 feet tall. Small white flowers in spring are followed by flavorful summertime fruit. These berries are most often powder blue but can also be black, red, or (rarely) white. The leaves turn attractive shades in fall.

Blueberries in Fall

Lowbush blueberries are responsible for perhaps the most dramatic blueberry display on the continent when the famed "blueberry barrens" light up the hills with smoldering red color. The intense crimson, orange, burgundy, and scarlet colors make the hillsides look like volcanoes spilling hot red lava down the slopes. Almost all blueberries, wherever they grow, have attractive fall foliage turning shades of orange and red.

Where to Find Blueberries

Blueberries grow in many areas across North America, from the Pacific Northwest to the South, Midwest, and Northeast.

- The black huckleberry or mountain blueberry *(V. membranaceum)* grows from about 1 to 6 feet tall along roadways, clear-cuts, and burned areas in a large area of the northern Rocky Mountains. The plants prefer locations about 1 mile in elevation.
- The Cascade huckleberry *(V. deliciosum)* thrives in the cool wet alpine meadows and evergreen forests of the Cascade Range and neighboring areas of Washington and British Columbia. The plants are often less than 2 feet tall and prefer the shores of ponds or wetlands above 2,000 feet.
- Bilberries *(V. myrtillus, V. caespitosum, V. uliginosum)* are true blueberries but different enough to be lumped into a subgroup all their own. They grow in many places and conditions, from the Pacific Coast, across the Rockies, through the Great Lakes, to New England.
- Whortleberries *(V. parvifolium, V. scoparium)* thrive in many areas of western North America, from Alaska south to California and east to

Shrub Stuff

Perhaps no other plant has so many names as the blueberry. The list includes *blueberry, huckleberry, sparkleberry, whortleberry, cowberry,* and *bilberry.* Blueberries were an important food source for Native Americans, who dried the berries and used them in cooking and mixed with meat and fat to make a food called pemmican.

Utah, Wyoming, and the Canadian Great Plains. The berries of some species are bright red.

- The hillside blueberry *(V. pallidum)* grows most abundantly in the southern Appalachians and Ozarks but can be found from New England west to Minnesota and south to Georgia and Oklahoma. It prefers rocky hillsides, where it grows beneath pines, hickory, post oak, and black oak.
- The rabbiteye blueberry *(V. ashei)* grows in an arc across the South, from North Carolina to the Mississippi River. It thrives in the understory beneath pine or mixed hardwood-pine forests. The plant gets its name because the immature fruit resembles a rabbit's eye.
- The highbush blueberry *(V. corymbosum)* is frequently seen in large plantations throughout its range, which reaches from Nova Scotia west to Illinois and south to Florida and Texas. The plants grow most abundantly in wetlands such as bogs, swamps, and marshes, as well as along slow streams and rivers. Look for them growing out over the water on the shores of backcountry lakes.
- The lowbush blueberry *(V. angustifolium)* grows from Labrador west to Manitoba and south to Illinois, West Virginia, and New England. It grows as an understory plant beneath pines, maples, and red oak but truly thrives in open treeless areas called blueberry barrens. You can admire the barrens in many states, but the finest show is the hill country of coastal Maine.

The Difference between Blueberries and Huckleberries

In many parts of North America, *huckleberry* is the preferred name for the blueberry. In other areas a dark-fruited blueberry is called a huckleberry. And in still other regions, the huckleberry and blueberry are totally different plants. Here's the way to keep everything straight.

To botanists the blueberry and huckleberry are completely separate plants, blueberries belonging to the genus *Vaccinium* and huckleberries to *Gaylussacia*. The fruits of blueberries have a star-shaped pattern on the base of the berry and soft seeds inside. Huckleberries are smooth and have very hard stony seeds inside. True huckleberries grow in eastern North America. Out west, blueberries are called huckleberries because that's what folks do and they've been doing it for generations.

Burning Bush | *Euonymus alatus*

Burning bush has upright winged branches that weep at the tips, giving the plant a broad vase shape. The plants can grow to more than 10 feet tall with small, medium green to dark green leaves. Tiny greenish flowers appear in spring, followed in late summer by brightly colored scarlet-red berries that ripen when the foliage begins to change.

Burning Bush in Fall

Burning bush thrives in a range of conditions, from full sun to nearly full shade and dry soils to wet. The foliage of plants growing in shady locations is pale pink to rose colored. Burning bush plants growing in full sun are spectacular, with fiery crimson leaves that seem to radiate a molten glow. Although both the foliage and berries are bright red, they are distinctive shades of red, the berries shining against a backdrop only slightly less intense.

Where to Find Burning Bush

Burning bush is native to Asia and was introduced to North America as an ornamental shrub in the 1860s. It is planted extensively along highways, especially near bridge abutments and exits; alongside homes, it is used around buildings or as a hedge. In the East and Midwest, the plant has naturalized in pastures, open forests, and prairies.

Shrub Stuff

The common name burning bush comes from the plant's hot-red fall foliage, a reference to the biblical tale (recounted in the book of Exodus) of Moses, who saw a bush alight with fire but not being burned.

Dogwood, Flowering | *Cornus florida*

Even people who don't notice trees notice this beauty. Flowering dogwood is native to much of the eastern United States and southern Ontario. The distinctive oval green leaves are prominently veined and often slightly curled. In spring clusters of tiny flowers are surrounded by large, showy white bracts. In some trees the bracts are tinted with pink. In fall the tips of the twigs hold small clusters of scarlet berries.

Flowering Dogwood in Fall

In fall flowering dogwood leaves change from green to burgundy, orange, red, and purple. The tips of dogwood branches turn up, appearing to be a colorful leafy cloud suspended above the forest floor. At the same time that the leaves change, clusters of berries near the branch tips ripen to a glossy scarlet-red that further brightens the fall display.

Where to Find Flowering Dogwood

Flowering dogwood is an understory tree growing in the shade of white, red, and black oaks, sweetgum, sassafras, and tulip tree. Dogwoods are solitary trees and can be found scattered through moist, open forests. Many parks, botanical gardens, and arboretums have gardens dedicated to dogwoods, including the National Arboretum of the United States in Washington, D.C.

DOGWOOD FAMILY

Shrub Stuff

Flowering dogwood was one of the favorite plants of two famous Virginians: George Washington, who planted the trees at his Mount Vernon home, and Thomas Jefferson, who grew them at Monticello.

Hornbeam, American (Ironwood)

Carpinus caroliniana

This small, handsome tree has smooth gray bark and a sinuous, muscular texture to the trunk and branches. The tidy framework of spreading branches is attractive, giving the tree a refined appearance. The leaves are dark green with a rough texture and coarse teeth along the margins. In spring the wiry "flowers," called catkins, hang from the branches like dozens of snippets of knitting yarn. In late summer the tree bears winged green fruit similar to hops, the plant used to flavor beer.

Hornbeam in Fall

Hornbeam leaves are compellingly attractive all by themselves; when set against the tree's rack of sinuous branches, the display is just that much more beautiful. In fall hornbeam leaves change from dark green to a number of colors, depending on where the plant grows. Some trees bear bright yellow leaves, whereas others have foliage of orange-yellow. In a few specimens the leaves turn a smoldering burnt orange.

Where to Find Hornbeam

Hornbeam is native to much of the eastern United States and extreme southeastern Canada. It prefers shady places and thrives in moist river margins, on streambanks, and on the shores of lakes and ponds. In the South the tree is found in company with holly, magnolia, gum trees, and red maples. In the North hornbeam grows as an understory plant beneath pines, oaks, maples, and basswood.

Shrub Stuff

Native Americans called hornbeam by the name Otantahrteweh, or "lean tree," in reference to the lean, muscular appearance of the trunk.

Juneberries (Shadbush) | *Amelanchier* spp.

Juneberries are small trees, from 5 to 30 feet tall, that thrive in the hardwood forests throughout much of eastern North America. In spring their slender gray branches are covered with dainty white flowers that open just as the leaves begin to expand. In June the trees bear small black berries, similar to blueberries, that are relished by many types of birds.

Juneberries in Fall

Juneberries have small oval leaves that turn vivid orange-scarlet in fall. The shape and size of the trees, combined with their bright-colored foliage, allow juneberries to stand out against the backdrop of hills and forest. Juneberries that grow in the forest understory where there is less sunlight have more muted colors but are still outstanding.

Where to Find Juneberries

Juneberries can grow just about anywhere but prefer well-drained slopes and banks near ponds, streams, and lakes throughout their range. They also thrive on the open crests and flanks of hills and ridges, as well as along the edges of fields, pastures, and forest clearings. They are solitary trees but are abundantly scattered through the woods.

ROSE FAMILY

Tree Facts

Juneberry is called shadbush, especially in New England, where the spring shad run in area rivers is an anticipated annual event. Shadbush is so named because it blooms when the shad run begins, the traditional signal for fishermen to head to the riverbanks.

Redbud | *Cercis canadensis*

Eastern redbud is a small tree normally growing to about 25 feet tall with thin, heart-shaped leaves. In spring, before the leaves emerge, the branches are smothered with misty pink blossoms. In fall the delicate green foliage warms to chromium yellow and gold, like diffuse beacons beaming throughout the woods.

Redbud in Fall

The glossy green redbud leaves turn bright molten gold in fall. The small size of redbud trees limits the magnitude of each specimen's individual foliage display. Redbud is often found growing amid flowering dogwood, wild plum, and other small, colorful trees. Together they create colorful leafy bouquets of yellow, orange, red, and violet that add color to the understory.

Where to Find Redbud

Eastern redbud grows from the Gulf States north to southern Minnesota and Pennsylvania. The tree grows in a wide variety of habitats, from Texas savanna to prairie and many types of forests. It is common at the edges of fields, along fencerows, and in forests, where it prefers ravines or the banks of streams and ponds. Redbud and flowering dogwood are frequent companions.

Redbud is a popular landscape tree and often adorns prominent positions in yards, botanical gardens, parks, college campuses, and even parking lots.

PEA FAMILY

Shrub Stuff

For centuries people have used the pinkish flowers of redbud as food wherever the plant grows. Most references have the flowers being used as an addition to salads, but some include eating the blossoms as a snack right from the tree.

Virginia Creeper | *Parthenocissus quinquefolia*

Virginia creeper is a vigorous vine that grows up the trunks and through the canopies of trees. It also covers the ground of open woods. Virginia creeper has distinctive leaves arranged in a whorl of five leaflets and climbs by using tiny suckers at the end of threadlike tendrils to grasp the tree.

Virginia Creeper in Fall

Few plants can match the display of Virginia creeper in fall. The vines cover tree trunks with crimson wildfire and blanket the forest floor like beds of glowing coals. The vines turn color before most trees, and the intense color amid the green landscape is an awe-inspiring sight. In shade the leaf color is less intense, changing to a pale rose-pink.

Where to Find Virginia Creeper

Virginia creeper is common throughout much of eastern North America and grows in many types of open woods, from pine groves to hardwood forest. It grows well on sunny roadsides and along the edges of hiking trails. Virginia creeper is also a popular landscape plant and can be found in yards and gardens climbing over stone walls, rambling over fences, or clinging to trellises and arbors.

Shrub Stuff

A near relative of Virginia creeper, Boston ivy has three-lobed leaves and is a very common landscape vine covering the sides of brick or stone buildings in many cities and towns. The leaves of Boston ivy—the namesake of the Ivy League colleges—are also attractive in fall, turning complex shades of red and orange.

Witch-Hazel | *Hamamelis virginiana*

Witch-hazel is a small straggly tree or shrub usually about 10 feet tall with oval, deeply veined leaves. In fall, often after the leaves have fallen, the branches are decorated with clusters of bright yellow, spidery flowers.

Witch-Hazel in Fall

Witch-hazel is one of those trees small enough to be sometimes encountered at eye level, making the saffron foliage easy to appreciate. In fall its leaves turn from green to shades of yellowish gold, often with deeper tones along the veins. Non-native species used for landscaping also have yellow foliage, with some offering leaves that turn reddish gold.

Where to Find Witch-Hazel

Witch-hazel is native to eastern North America, from the Gulf of the Saint Lawrence River southwest to southern Minnesota and south to the Gulf States. It prefers wet, cool areas such as streambanks and the shores of ponds, where its golden leaves are beautiful reflected in the water.

Shrub Stuff

The scientific name for witch-hazel, *Hamamelis,* means "to bear flowers and fruit at the same time," a reference to the plant's shedding seed and blossoming simultaneously in fall. The *witch* of *witch-hazel* refers to the use of the plant's forked twigs by people called water witches to discover the location of groundwater. *Hazel* is in reference to witch-hazel's resemblance to European winter hazel *(Corylopsis* spp.).

Fall Foliage in
Cities and Towns

Callery Pear | *pyrus calleryana*

The Callery pear is the most commonly grown ornamental pear. The tree is native to China and has an attractive symmetrical crown of upright branches. In spring Callery pear is smothered with white flowers similar to apple blossoms. The fruits are brown and are the size and shape of marbles.

Callery Pear in Fall

In fall the Callery pear puts on a gorgeous show, with foliage that turns dark shades of burgundy and red. The leaves of some varieties are brighter red, whereas others are reddish with a coppery cast. The pleasing foliage color is displayed nicely against the tree's symmetrical form.

Where to Find Callery Pear

Callery pears are favorites for lining Main Street, where the uniform shape against the backdrop of storefronts makes every town seem like home. They can also be found in botanical gardens, arboretums, parks, and college campuses.

Tree Facts

A beautiful variety of Callery pear is the Bradford pear, a thornless type discovered in a batch of seeds collected by plant explorer Frank N. Meyer in China. Meyer died in China but the seeds found their way to America, where they were planted and then largely forgotten. Thirty-two years later one tree was particularly handsome and was named the Bradford pear. That one tree is the source of all Bradford pears everywhere.

Franklin Tree | *Franklinia alatamaha*

The Franklin tree is small, about 15 feet tall, with upright, slender branches. The glossy dark green leaves are a beautiful touch to the garden, expanding to about 6 inches long and gracefully curved inward at the sides. In late summer to early fall, the tree bears large solitary flowers, similar to camellia, with white petals.

Franklin Tree in Fall

In fall the large, narrow, dark green leaves of the Franklin tree transform into rich red foliage that shines like the finest mahogany polished to a gloss. Some years the flowers still cling to the branches as the leaves turn color; the showy blossoms seem to float amid the leafy backdrop.

Where to Find Franklin Tree

Most of the Franklin trees in the world grow in parks, botanical gardens, and private yards in a belt from Ohio east to Philadelphia and north to eastern Massachusetts; eastern Pennsylvania has the greatest concentration of trees.

TEA FAMILY

Tree Facts

In the late summer of 1765, botanists John and William Bartram explored the Alatamaha River Valley in Georgia. There they discovered a beautiful tree in full bloom. They named the tree after their friend Benjamin Franklin and brought cuttings and seeds back to Philadelphia. By 1803 the tree had disappeared from the wild but still grows in gardens and yards.

Ginkgo (Maidenhair Tree) | *Ginkgo biloba*

Ginkgo is a strongly upright tree to 100 feet tall, with light gray, furrowed bark and distinctive fan-shaped greenish yellow leaves. Young trees have sparse branches, but older ones are full and attractive. In fall the female trees may bear fruit that contain edible "nuts" (they smell like rancid butter when old).

Ginkgo Trees in Fall

Ginkgo trees are conifers, like pines. Fossils indicate that ginkgo trees have been growing on Earth for more than 250 million years, making them some of the oldest trees in existence. In fall the fan-shaped leaves turn from pale green to butter yellow.

Where to Find Ginkgo Trees

Ginkgo trees tolerate pollution and are not fussy about growing conditions. These traits have made them popular in urban areas. You can find them in nearly every city and town. Some places have so many ginkgo trees that the fall display is quite spectacular, including:

- *Washington, D.C.* Department of Agriculture, Capitol Hill.
- *Philadelphia.* Longwood Gardens, Bartram's Garden.
- *New York City.* Brooklyn Botanic Garden, Greenwich Village, Central Park.

Other locations include these college campuses: University of Virginia, Virginia Tech, University of Missouri, and University of Iowa.

Tree Facts

Ginkgo trees were once native to a small area of China, but are now extinct in the wild. The name *ginkgo* is a Chinese word that means "silver apricot," referring to the shape and color of the fruit. Ginkgo is also called maidenhair tree because the leaves resemble those of maidenhair fern. The tree is extensively used in herbal medicine and is said to improve memory and increase oxygen to the brain.

Katsura Tree | *Cercidiphyllum japonicum*

This stately shade tree native to Japan and China reaches about 75 feet tall and 50 feet wide. The rounded heart-shaped leaves—sometimes with a hint of blush—have a simple elegance, giving the tree a soft, uncomplicated appearance. Tiny red flowers appear in spring before the leaves.

Katsura Tree in Fall

The katsura tree gathers all of autumn's colors—yellow, orange, red, and coppery bronze—and displays them on each leaf. Rather than just appearing in spots and patches across the leaf, the colors on katsura leaves also seem layered, producing an effect of depth as well as intensity. Katsura trees change color before most other trees, making them easy to pick out in the landscape.

Where to Find Katsura Tree

Katsura trees are now commonly available in the nursery trade, and smaller specimens can be found in many yards. To see large trees, visit the campuses of land grant universities or botanical gardens. The trees are especially tolerant of urban conditions and are becoming increasingly popular along streets and in city parks.

KATSURA TREE FAMILY

Tree Facts

In China and Japan, where the katsura is native, finding large specimens is easy. In North America, however, they are still newcomers, although there are some large individuals. Perhaps the largest katsura in North America is a century-old tree at the Morris Arboretum of the University of Pennsylvania. This multistemmed tree is 67 feet tall with a canopy that spans about 90 feet.

Kousa Dogwood | *Cornus kousa*

The kousa dogwood is a small tree from Japan and Korea growing about 20 feet tall with a naturally neat, tapered shape that looks as if it has been carefully pruned. The leaves are similar to other dogwoods but with wavy edges. Kousa dogwood flowers in June, a few weeks later than the flowering dogwood, with large flowers in colors from white to red.

Kousa Dogwood in Fall

Kousa dogwood trees are most often planted in open areas where they are easy to see, even from a distance. In fall the leaves turn from green to shades of rich maroon, crimson, and russet orange, holding their colors for weeks before dropping.

Where to Find Kousa Dogwood

The kousa dogwood is common in yards and parks from central New England west to the Great Plains and south to around the Gulf Coast. It's also popular in the Pacific coastal region. Many botanical gardens and arboretums have dogwood collections that highlight these trees and produce stunning displays in fall. A beautiful example is the dogwood garden at the United States National Arboretum in Washington, D.C.

Tree Facts

For decades Dr. Elwin Orton, a plant breeder at Rutgers University, worked to produce hybrids of kousa and flowering dogwoods. In 1993 these hybrids were released under the name Stellar Series. The plants are similar to the kousa in shape and flower, with some of the pliancy and gracefulness so loved in flowering dogwood.

Maple, Japanese | *Acer palmatum*

Some Japanese maple trees have red foliage all season long, but many have green leaves that turn bright, cheerful colors in fall, the display becoming the centerpiece of the garden. The Japanese maple is native to eastern Asia and features maple-shaped leaves in a wide variety of styles. The trees are typically less than 25 feet tall, with smooth gray bark.

Japanese Maple in Fall

In fall the foliage changes from green to red, yellow, orange, and every shade in between. Often the green is reluctant to leave and remains as an undertone on portions of the leaf blade like a dying echo. The leaves are made more attractive because the fall shades tend to run together, creating their own sunset.

Where to Find Japanese Maple

The Japanese maple can be found just about everywhere, from back-yards to botanical gardens. If you want a lot of Japanese maples in one place, visit the Washington Park Arboretum at the University of Washington in Seattle, with the largest collection in the country—about ninety varieties. Japanese maples highlight the Japanese garden at the Missouri Botanical Garden in St. Louis. The Hershey Rose Garden and Arboretum in Hershey, Pennsylvania, also has a magnificent collection. Other destinations include the Maxwell Arboretum (University of Nebraska, Lincoln), the J. C. Raulston Arboretum (North Carolina State University), and the National Arboretum of the United States (Washington, D.C.).

Tree Facts

The Japanese maple was introduced to England and North America around 1820.

Stewartia | *Stewartia* spp.

Stewartia can have one stem or many, with the branches and trunk wrapped in a rich cinnamon-colored bark that gracefully peels in tight curls. In midsummer the branches are adorned with beautiful camellia-like white flowers framed by glossy dark green leaves.

Stewartia in Fall

Stewartia trees are native to both Asia and North America. In fall the dark green leaves turn shades of maroon, red, scarlet, and orange. Some species, such as Korean Stewartia, also add a little yellow to the mix. The leaves, similar to a Franklin tree, have a gentle upward curve that can intensify the display. The curl in the shiny leaf seems to amplify any light striking the foliage, creating areas of more intense color.

Where to Find Stewartia

Stewartia is a favorite tree of botanical gardens, arboretums, and college campuses. Readily available from nurseries, it is not yet very common in backyards and parks. Stewartia collections can be found at many horticultural institutions, including the Hoyt Arboretum (Portland, Oregon) and Arnold Arboretum (Boston, Massachusetts). Native Stewartia trees can most likely be seen in the wild along coastal South Carolina and the border of Florida and Alabama (silky Stewartia), also in the border area of Tennessee, North Carolina, and Georgia (mountain Stewartia).

TEA FAMILY

Tree Facts

The name *Stewartia* honors John Stuart (1713–1792), who was third earl of Bute, prime minister of England in 1762, and a close adviser to King George III. The original spelling of *Stewartia* was *Stuartia*.

Bottlebrush Buckeye | *Aesculus parviflora*

Bottlebrush buckeye is a shrubby 8-foot-tall relative of horse chestnut. The plant spreads freely into an attractive if impenetrable mass. The large leaves are dark green and slightly droopy, like dozens of emerald umbrellas on the branches. In summer tall spikes of delicate white flowers point skyward. In fall round "buckeyes," which look similar to chestnuts, appear.

Bottlebrush Buckeye in Fall

In fall the large leaves of bottlebrush buckeye turn a uniform golden yellow so attractive that they seem to give off warmth. The plants can grow anywhere and endure anything, making them reliable even in shady places.

Where to Find Bottlebrush Buckeye

Bottlebrush buckeye is native to a small region of the southeast United States but is grown from the Pacific Northwest to Maine. The plant is commonly available in nurseries and can increasingly be found in yards and gardens. Bottlebrush buckeye is most often encountered in botanical gardens, arboretums, college campuses, and parks.

HORSE CHESTNUT FAMILY

Shrub Stuff

Very large specimens of bottlebrush buckeye are fairly common in the South as well as in long-established botanical gardens. The plants are characterized by the spread of the shrub rather than height. The Arnold Arboretum in Boston has a massive specimen. The High Hampton Inn of Cashiers, North Carolina, boasts a plant about 20 feet tall and twice that in width.

Chokeberry, Red | *Aronia arbutifolia*

This moderate-size shrub is densely branched with a roughly conical shape. It spreads easily, creating nearly impenetrable tangles. The dark green oblong leaves have a pointed tip and small teeth along the edge. Small white blossoms cover the bush in spring and yield bright red berries that ripen in fall.

Red Chokeberry in Fall

Although it is true that the berries are quite unpalatable, this shrub does have a redeeming quality: its outstanding fall color. During summer red chokeberry is pretty nondescript, fading into the green background of gardens, yards, and shrub borders. In fall its personality abruptly changes—the leaves turn baked-enamel red as hundreds of scarlet berries hang from the branches. The effect is stunning.

Where to Find Red Chokeberry

Red chokeberry is most often found growing in dense thickets in open areas such as ridgetops as well as moist areas of lower elevation. The plant can be found from parts of southern Canada south to eastern Texas and Florida. Red chokeberry is planted in many botanical gardens and arboretums. It is sometimes used in mass plantings along highway medians and near overpasses.

Shrub Stuff

If you want to add red chokeberry to your own garden or backyard, look for a variety called Brilliantissima. This selection is an improvement over the species as it has bigger, more abundant fruit and shiny darker green leaves that turn brilliant red in fall.

Fothergilla, Dwarf | *Fothergilla gardenii*

This low-growing shrub is native to the Southeast, from North Carolina to Alabama and Florida. It thrives in moist woodlands and swampy areas in company with tupelo and sweetgum trees. In spring it bears white, sweetly fragrant flowers that look like rounded bottle-brushes at the tips of the branches. The green summer foliage has a hint of blue and looks similar to that of witch-hazel.

Dwarf Fothergilla in Fall

You might think it is easy to overlook a plant that grows only about 3 feet tall. But walk into a garden in fall where dwarf fothergilla is growing and you can't miss it—it steals the show. In fall the foliage of this little shrub transforms into infinite combinations of red, orange, and yellow. The colors are so complex and vibrant, they seem to blend and change right before your eyes.

Where to Find Dwarf Fothergilla

Though native to the South, dwarf fothergilla adapts to areas far outside its native range and can be found in gardens from New England to the Pacific Northwest. It is common in parks, botanical gardens, and many yards and gardens.

WITCH-HAZEL FAMILY

Shrub Stuff

Some dwarf fothergilla plants have more intense fall coloration than others. To light up your yard every fall, plant a variety called "Mount Airy." This variety is widely available from nurseries and has been selected specifically for its consistent and brilliant fall display.

Smokebush | *Cotinus coggygria*

There are only two species of smokebush in the world, one native to Europe and Asia and the other to eastern America. Both have round to oval leaves and dense upright branches that produce a canopy of foliage that billows like a cumulous cloud in a summer sky. In summer characteristic sprays of misty, greenish lavender flowers appear above the foliage, draping the plant in a unique gossamer veil.

Smokebush in Fall

Few plants exhibit such uniform beauty in fall as smokebush. The leaves quickly turn from pale green to smoldering shades of yellow-orange dipped in lava red. Older specimens are often stout and rounded; they're simply beautiful plants, dense with color, having a dignified presence. Young plants have to grow out of an awkward stage but still produce a fine fall display.

Where to Find Smokebush

American smokebush is rare in the wild, surviving in a few locations of the southern United States along river bluffs, ravines, and rocky hillsides. The Asian/European smokebush is a very common landscape plant, especially the varieties that sport purple foliage from spring through fall. These varieties, besides being horribly overused, have no useful fall color.

Shrub Stuff

Also called yellowwood and smoke tree, the American smokebush was nearly destroyed when many of the trees, especially the largest ones, were cut down in the nineteenth and early twentieth centuries to make an orange dye from the wood.

Staghorn Sumac | *Rhus* spp.

Staghorn sumac grows about 20 feet tall with palmlike leaves. The name refers to the velvety upper branches—like a buck's antlers in spring. In late summer spires of fuzzy red fruit ripen, clinging to the branches through winter.

Caution: Poison sumac is an uncommon shrub or small tree of swamps and wetlands. *The leaves have a smooth edge rather than toothed, and the berries are white rather than red.*

Sumac in Fall

In fall sumac trees erupt with intense red-hot color. The tropical-looking leaves become simply brilliant, turning shades of gold, amber-orange, and crimson-red. Staghorn sumac often grows with flowers such as goldenrods and asters. The combination of leaves, foliage, and flowers is unforgettable.

Where to Find Sumac

Sumac likes to grow in areas that have been disturbed or abandoned, such as roadsides and trails, at the edge of forests, and in clear-cuts and unused fields throughout much of eastern North America. Some types, such as fragrant sumac and cutleaf staghorn sumac, are valued as ornamental shrubs and can be found in gardens, yards, parks, and arboretums throughout much of the continent.

Shrub Stuff

Years ago the spouts that were set into the maple trees in spring to direct the sap into the buckets were made of sumac. Each tap was carved from the branch of a sumac bush. Sumac wood has a spongy center pith that is easily poked out with a slender rod, resulting in a hollow tube through which the sap could run.

Viburnums | *Viburnum* spp.

Viburnums are showy shrubs that beautify the garden every season of the year. Many types bear snow-white rounded clusters of intensely fragrant blossoms in spring. From summer through fall clumps of attractive fruit ripen. And in the chill of autumn, the handsome foliage is washed with soft russet, red, and orange like the last breath of a sunset.

Viburnums in Fall

The predominant fall color of most viburnums is a warm red that seamlessly melts into secondary colors such as crimson, burnt orange, and burgundy. Many species and varieties also sport vivid red or yellow fruit that adds an extra accent.

Where to Find Viburnums

There are more than a hundred species of viburnums. Native species, such as arrowwood and American cranberry, add interest to woodland walks. The most spectacular displays and the most beautiful plants can often be found in and near major cities.

Viburnums are the mainstay of countless gardens, botanical gardens, college campuses, and city parks. They are often grouped together in shrub borders, placed along walkways, or used as foundation plantings around buildings—places where the fragrance of the blossoms can be easily appreciated. This placement also makes admiring their fall foliage that much easier. Some places to visit that have excellent exhibits include:

- Longwood Gardens, Kennett Square (Philadelphia), Pennsylvania.
- Dawes Arboretum, Newark, Ohio.
- Arnold Arboretum, Jamaica Plain (Boston), Massachusetts.
- Maxwell Arboretum, University of Nebraska, Lincoln, Nebraska.
- Holden Arboretum, Kirkland, Ohio.
- National Arboretum of the United States, Washington, D.C.

HONEYSUCKLE FAMILY

Shrub Stuff

The American cranberry bush has flat, white flowers in spring and clusters of bright red berries that last well into, and sometimes through, the winter. The berries make the garden attractive in the colder months and do resemble cranberries, but the flavor is what gives this shrub its name. The edible berries are flavorful but have a sour-tart bite that is certainly unique.

Bright Spots

Rules of the Road: How to See Fall Foliage Successfully

What does it mean to see fall foliage successfully? It means to enjoy the experience. Fall's peak is short-lived, and moments need to be seized. One of the best things about viewing fall foliage is that it doesn't happen just in one place. Unlike visiting a museum, fall foliage transforms the entire landscape. It is something to be enjoyed both coming and going. Here are some tips to make it the best experience possible.

Remember the camera and the film. Fall foliage season is a time of so much color that to remember it all requires that you take photographs. Whether you are a professional or a point-and-shooter, you'll be glad you took the time to save some moments of fall. Remember to look for shots with uniform lighting, and avoid dappled light.

Take your time. The splendor of fall foliage is not a secret, and the most colorful highways and back roads can be crowded. Weekends are the most congested times, midweek the least.

Time your trip. Foliage destinations will provide you with peak foliage times that denote when the most color can be seen. People tend to flock to destinations during the week of peak color, then disappear like frost on a warm morning. This leaves off-peak times, often the week before and week after peak, much less crowded.

Watch the weather. The weather can make or break a foliage excursion. As leaves turn, they are also getting ready to drop from the trees. If rain and wind are in the forecast as trees near peak, it is better to get out and see things *before* the storm rather than after.

Find color in towns as well as in the woods. Some of the most common landscape trees and shrubs turn stunning colors in fall. Other plants of yards and gardens come from lands thousands of miles away, and their colors can't be seen in the forests. If the back roads are crowded, come to the towns and cities, visit the botanical gardens, and walk the sidewalks. You'll find great color and probably great places to shop while you stop and enjoy the fall scenery.

New England

New England is one of those rare places that combines exquisite natural beauty, ever-present reminders of centuries of history, and unique culture. There are postcard villages with town greens, tree-lined colonial-style homes, and quaint shops. Covered bridges span white-water streams, and orchards of carefully tended trees sparkle with ripening red apples. Dairy cows graze on rolling pastures beside old red barns and silos. Miles and miles of stone walls follow winding country roads, and the horizon is filled with the profiles of ancient weathered mountains that rise above the valleys like silent guardians.

To this add some of the most intense and abundant fall foliage in the world, and you'll see why an autumn visit to New England is an experience that is unparalleled.

The uniform brilliance of New England's foliage is due to a chain of fortunate circumstances. The region lies along a band of latitude where day length seasonally increases and decreases to produce the best color. The climate is cool but moderated by the nearby ocean to reduce temperature extremes that can damage leaves and leaf color. Precipitation is near optimal, soils are good, and the forest is extensive, covering a large majority of the region. Finally, the woods are often a blend of many different species that produce strong colors in a wide variety of shades.

New England isn't a large place, but it is so full of things to see and do that visitors cannot help but linger.

Littleton, New Hampshire

To get the most out of New England, take it slow so you can enjoy the people as well as the fall scenery. New Englanders are thoughtful people with wonderful stories to share that add color to an already colorful destination.

Connecticut

Beyond the cities are vast protected forests where oaks, hickories, maples, and tulip trees grow. A walk in the woods here is more than a visual treat—you can *smell* the fall leaves in the air. Oaks have a rich earthy scent; the maples, a heady sweet odor. It is simply delightful.

Expect peak color in Connecticut's northwest hills as early as mid-October, but it may hold off a week. Peak in the rest of the state is generally the last week in October to the first week in November. Points in Connecticut are close to New York City, Boston, Hartford, Springfield, and Albany.

HIKES WITH A VIEW

River Walk on the Appalachian Trail: This 5-mile section of trail is the longest river walk on the entire Appalachian Trail. It runs from the end of River Road in Kent to Cornwall Bridge. The mostly flat trail traces a path through varied and colorful woods along the western bank of the picturesque Housatonic River. Enjoy the miles of woods with maples, birch, and ash all around. You'll also find groves of sassafras with their yellow leaves.

White Memorial Conservation Center, just south of Litchfield village, is a wonderful place to enjoy the fall foliage. Check out the 1.2-mile boardwalk trail around Little Pond.

Sleeping Giant State Park is in Hamden, across from the campus of Quinnipiac University. The path up the mountain is hard packed and winds through rich forests and dark basalt cliffs. At the top is a stone castle with stunning views out toward Long Island Sound.

DRIVING TOUR

Northwest Hills: From the center of Litchfield, follow Route 202 west past White Memorial (see "Hikes with a View"). From here to New Preston the road is scenic, with plentiful brightly colored woods. Continue south from New Preston along the beautiful Aspetuck River to New Milford and the junction of Route 7. Turn north on Route 7, through Bulls Bridge and Kent. From Kent continue north on Route 7 to Cornwall Bridge, home of

---

Sweet Thoughts

As you pour maple syrup over a stack of hot pancakes, is your mind telling you that anything this sweet and delicious has to be bad for you? Relax. Even though maple syrup is almost entirely composed of sugar, it is surprisingly low in calories. For example, corn syrup contains sixty calories per tablespoon, honey has sixty-four calories, and brown sugar comes out at fifty-one. The same amount of maple syrup has just forty calories. Maple syrup is also organic, fat-free, and contains no preservatives or additives. Finally, pure maple syrup contains many vitamins and minerals, including as much calcium as whole milk.

Autumn reflection on the Salmon River, Colchester, Connecticut

one of the most beautiful covered bridges in the country. The one-lane bridge spans the Housatonic River where the stream is a tumble of thrilling white water. From Cornwall Bridge continue north through Falls Village and the junction of Route 63. Take Route 63 south through expansive woods and fields, passing Goshen along the way back to Litchfield. For other interesting trips, try **Castle Craig and the Hanging Hills,** located off West Main Street in Meriden's acclaimed Hubbard Park, or **Scenic Byway Route 169,** which travels a north-south route through extreme eastern Connecticut nearly midway between Hartford and Providence. The eastern hills are known for apple orchards and small towns still rich in colonial ambience.

Massachusetts

Massachusetts will capture your heart from the moment you begin to explore its shores and mountains. You'll find the classic beaches, lighthouses, and harbor towns of Cape Cod and the islands, of course, but the Bay State also has some of the most beautiful foliage in the country, dressing the Worcester Hills and the Berkshire Mountains in timeless color each autumn. Here the colored forests that cover the mountains and valleys are joined like bolts of bright cloth into a quilt of resplendent beauty. Perhaps that's why so many people make these hills their getaway for weekends. Life is slower here, and the relaxed pace increases your enjoyment of the area's treasures. An unhurried stroll down a village lane lined with old maple trees becomes a memory that will refresh you for years to come. The invigorating hike along a trail in the Berkshires is even more exhilarating as you come to a rocky overlook thousands of feet above a forest of fall colors below. The landscape is a wonderful combination of ancient mountains and valleys with foliage that boasts vivid colors and strikingly clear shades, a breathtaking experience.

The foliage season peaks in Massachusetts in early to late October, with some southwestern spots holding color into early November.

DRIVING TOURS

Mount Greylock is the state's highest peak at 3,487 feet. From the junction of Routes 8 and 7 in Pittsfield, follow Route 7 north 5.8 miles to North Main Street in Lanesborough. Turn right onto North Main Street (which becomes Rockwell Road once within Mount Greylock State Reservation), and travel 8.3 miles to the junction with Notch Road high on Mount Greylock. Just inside the reservation is a visitor center with a grand view south over the central Berkshire lakes. At Notch Road turn right onto Summit Road, and follow it 0.9 mile past some vertigo overlooks to the main parking area.

The mountaintop is beautiful, with the graceful memorial tower rising from the summit. The Appalachian Trail crosses the summit near Bascom Lodge, a cozy shelter from the omnipresent wind. A walk near the tower offers many stunning views into the valley about 2,000 feet below.

Worcester Hills and Quabbin Reservoir: From Worcester take Interstate 190 north to exit 5, then follow Route 140 north 2 miles to Route 62. Take Route 62 west, and enjoy a gorgeous country drive. In Barre continue west on combined Routes 32/122. In Petersham follow Route 122 as it wraps around the northern end of Quabbin Reservoir, a huge lake with wide bays prying into the hills and dotted with wooded islands. This area was once home to small villages now drowned or abandoned. The area has gone wild with bald eagles and black bears. There have even been sightings of cougars. At the junction with Route 202, turn south and follow the road as it traces a path along the lake's western shore. At the reservoir's south end, take Route 9 east back to Worcester.

Preserving Autumn Leaves

Beauty is treasured in part because it is so fleeting. The striking beauty of autumn leaves lasts only hours before the colors begin to fade. Sharp shades age into muted tones before evaporating into a mass of featureless brown. As a photograph captures a moment in time, preserved autumn leaves keep fond memories fresh and vibrant. Preserving leaves can be a fun family project.

There are many ways to preserve fall foliage—from ironing between sheets of wax paper to zapping them in a microwave. The following method uses glycerin and water and preserves the leaves while keeping them soft and flexible.

Find a glass or plastic container large enough to comfortably fit your leafy treasures. Lay the leaves in the container. Mix glycerin and water at a rate of one part glycerin to three parts water, making enough solution to cover the leaves. Gently pour the glycerin and water solution over the leaves, being sure all leaf surfaces are covered. Seal the container and place it in a dimly lit room for one to three weeks. The leaves are ready if the color appears uniform from the central vein out to the leaf edge. Remove the leaves and dry on newspaper for a few days.

Monument Mountain: This is a snow-white mountain with sterling views. Located at the northern end of Great Barrington, Monument Mountain is a long ridge of crystal-white quartzite that offers hikers a range of views from the Connecticut hills in the south to Mount Greylock in the north. It is also where, in 1850, Herman Melville sat out a thunderstorm chatting with Nathaniel Hawthorne about the latest novel he was writing: *Moby Dick*.

From the parking lot on Route 7, the most popular hike heads north, follows the base of a huge boulder slope, and passes a shallow cave hidden behind a waterfall. The trail then swings south and scrambles to the ridge crest, which is covered with bare white bedrock and wind-stunted trees. The path straddles the ridge and comes to the signature features of the mountain: Squaw Peak and Devil's Pulpit. Squaw Peak is a long cliff of fractured stone that drops hundreds of feet to the forest below. The view from here, especially south, is extraordinary. Devil's Pulpit is a tower of rock that separated from Squaw Peak millennia ago. The path descends, sometimes steeply, to an old carriage road that continues to the south end of the mountain. Just off the trail is the monument of Monument Mountain, a pile of stones that was a sacred place of the Mahican people who lived here. This moderate to strenuous hike is about 2.5 miles round-trip.

Hurlburt Hill and Bartholomew's Cobble: This is an easy hike through hay fields and hardwoods to a sweeping view of the Berkshires. Head south down the gravel road a few yards, then turn right into a grassy field. The easy path gently climbs through a series of open hay fields bordered by bands of hardwood forest. The trail steepens just before entering a very large field studded with dozens of bluebird boxes. Bluebirds and swallows

Ginkgo

Wachusett Mountain is a little more than 2,000 feet high but tall enough to afford long views of forests and towns all the way to the Boston skyline. From Princeton on Route 62, head north 2.4 miles on Mountain Road to trailhead. The **Mountain House Trail** is unmarked but easy to follow. The 1-mile moderate path is eroded and steep in places as it climbs the mountain to parallel the summit road before reaching the top and all the views you could want. A drivable road runs to the summit. Wachusett Mountain Park Headquarters is on Mountain Road in Princeton.

Vermont

Ask for one place associated with fall foliage, and the most probable reply is "Vermont." The name *Vermont* derives from the French words meaning green mountains, and for much of the year, Vermont lives up to its name. But in the fall the green turns into an encompassing expanse of color that spills from the hilltops to the valley floors below. Every shade, tone, and hue—from intense yellow to burgundy-purple—can be found in the foliage. The color of the fall foliage in Vermont is magnified by the landscape: quaint town greens lined with sugar maple trees, covered bridges over whitewater streams, mountain views, rugged ravines, and waterfalls.

The forests of Vermont are as extensive as they are beautiful, covering the majority of the state. The most colorful trees are the most common and include maple, oak, birch, beech, and ash. Above about 3,200 feet and in northern Vermont, the hardwoods share the forest with evergreen spruce and balsam fir.

The foliage season begins in mid- to late September, when colors peak in the Northeast Kingdom through central Vermont. The remainder of the state, from the

sweep through the air, and bobolinks chase each other through the field. Deer often can be seen here, and bobcats like to walk the fencerows.

At the top is a bench and one of the best views in the Berkshires. The Taconics are to the west, and on a clear day, Mount Greylock, more than 60 miles away, can be seen. The foliage is mind-boggling—it covers everything with color from the mountains to the valleys. An interpretive display near the bench helps you to enjoy the annual hawk migration.

From the stop signs at the center of Ashley Falls (Route 7A), turn onto Rannapo Road and travel 0.9 mile to Weatogue Road. Turn onto Weatogue Road, and continue to the parking area and nature center 0.1 mile on the left.

Champlain Valley to the Massachusetts border, peaks from early to mid-October. Some years the southern valleys can peak from mid- to late October.

DRIVING TOUR

Route 100 is one very long and wonderfully scenic country road. It runs nearly the length of Vermont, from just north of the Massachusetts border to just south of Canada. Along the way are scores of country towns, ski resorts with fall foliage rides, country stores, gorgeous views, state parks, and the Green Mountain National Forest. The most popular section extends from the Routes 100 and 9 junction in Wilmington (southern Vermont) north to the Route 4 junction east of Rutland. The road has a lot of twists and turns, so people drive slowly anyway. During peak foliage—about the second and third week of October—it gets very crowded, and traffic slows down even more. So buy some maple syrup and apple cider, and enjoy the view.

Consider these drives as well:

• Route 9 from Bennington to Brattleboro in southern Vermont—over the spine of the Green Mountains with splendid views.

• Route 7A and Route 30 from Bennington to Middlebury—explores Green Mountain National Forest and the historic lower Champlain Valley in southwestern Vermont.

HIKES WITH A VIEW

Mount Equinox, at 3,816 feet, is the tallest peak in the Taconic Range and by far the most majestic. The mountain seems to stand alone, isolated from other summits and looming over the Battenkill Valley. Skyline Drive (toll road) winds up the southwest ridge to the summit and the Skyline Inn. A network of trails leave from the inn, including Lookout Rock Trail. This 0.8-mile round-

Vermont's Triple Crown

If you visit Vermont, it is required you sample three things: Vermont maple syrup, apple cider, and cheddar cheese. Vermonters don't say that their maple syrup is better than the syrup made elsewhere. They just say that it's the best. But is it really better? Well, much of this is personal preference, but Vermont law does demand that Vermont maple syrup exceed the federal standards most other states use.

Likewise, apple cider is more than apple juice. The best cider is a calculated blend of selected apple varieties that produces a cider with a balanced apple flavor. Vermont orchards often grow an abundance of apple varieties, so the cider presses produce exceptional cider.

You can count on Vermont for white cheese. Vermonters are of the mind that if cheese were meant to be orange, cows would be making orange milk. You won't find orange cheese in Vermont, but the cheese you do find is aged to excellence. If you're in northern Vermont near Montpelier, visit the Cabot Creamery for a taste of real Vermont cheddar.

trip walk descends the north ridge to Lookout Rock and views to Mount Ascutney, Monadnock, and the White Mountains of New Hampshire far on the horizon.

Mount Equinox is off Route 7 just south of Manchester Center in southwest Vermont. Also consider:

- Glastonbury Mountain and the Long Trail. This rugged 20-mile round-trip hike leads to the observation tower atop Glastonbury Mountain. The view from the top is absolutely breathtaking. A hiker's overnight shelter south of the summit makes this a viable weekend trip.

- Snake Mountain overlooking Lake Champlain, which was once called Grand View Mountain to honor the extraordinary vistas from the slopes and summit. This moderate 3.2-mile round-trip hike follows old logging and carriage roads to the top, where views all the way to the Adirondacks await. Snake Mountain is a great place to watch raptor migration too.

New Hampshire

Parts of New Hampshire, such as the Presidential Range, combine rugged beauty and bright fall foliage so effectively that they commonly head lists for the best fall destinations in the country. New Hampshire extends from the Atlantic coast all the way to the Canadian border and in elevation from sea level to more than 6,000 feet. Foliage peaks in the northern forests and at elevations above about 3,000 feet in late September. In the White Mountains the peak is from late September through mid-October, with the valleys a few days later. Much of the remainder of the state peaks from October 7 to October 21. The southern sections, including areas around Mount Monadnock, peak in late October, with some foliage along the coast hanging on into early November.

The main species to look for include sugar and red maples, ash, and paper, black, and yellow birches.

White Mountains: To view the ragged peaks and striking foliage of the Presidential Range, begin in Lincoln, and follow the Kancamangus Highway (Route 112) east. Follow Route 16 north, then turn left onto Route 302, which leads you through the magnificent cleft in the mountains called Crawford Notch. Continue to U.S. Highway 3, and head south to the amazing sights of Franconia Notch and back to Lincoln.

The Mount Washington Auto Road (toll) is the oldest man-made attraction in the United States. Beginning from Great Glen off Route 16 it ascends about 8 miles up Chandler Ridge to the summit of Mount Washington. Most days the summit is shrouded in fog, but the trip up the mountain is a continuous, spectacular view of mountains, valleys, and foliage.

The Train to the Clouds

The Cog Railway is the world's first mountain-climbing cog railway and chugs up a 3-mile, amazingly steep trestle to the top of New Hampshire's Mount Washington (800–922–8825). The base station and parking area are located off Route 302 at Bretton Woods. If a mountain-climbing train isn't your thing, try a ride on the **Hobo Train** out of Lincoln or the **Lake Winnipesaukee Scenic Train** departing from Meredith. Both trains run through areas of bright fall foliage.

The White Mountains are the tallest, most stunning mountains in the Northeast and have dozens of unforgettable trips of varying difficulties. Two relatively easy trips begin at the Appalachian Mountain Club's Pinkham Notch Camp off Route 16.

Square Ledge is a rocky mantle perched above Pinkham Notch with a beautiful view of Mount Washington. Cross Route 16 to **Lost Lake Trail.** After the bridge follow Square Ledge Trail up Wildcat Mountain for 0.5 mile to the breathtaking overlook.

For a longer walk, follow the wide trail called the Old Jackson Road (1.9 miles), which starts behind Joe Dodge Lodge. At the Mount Washington Auto Road, cross the road, and follow the Madison Gulf Trail 0.2 mile to a spur trail right that climbs 0.1 mile to the brushy outcrop called Lowe's Bald Spot. The view is stunning.

If you'd like to climb Mount Washington rather than just view it, hike up the demanding Tuckerman Ravine Trail from Pinkham Notch Camp. The trek travels about 4 miles up through Tuckerman Ravine to the summit of Mount Washington (6,288 feet), home of the worst weather in the world but the best view in New England when it's clear.

Maine

Maine is a beautiful place to visit, with hundreds of wilderness lakes and immense tracts of northern forest. The most stunning part of the state, especially during the foliage season, is the midcoast region, a swath of rugged shoreline from Brunswick in the south to Mount Desert Island in the north. The midcoast is home to numerous old-fashioned fishing villages, with small harbors dotted with lobster boats (in Maine, lobster red is a fall color). Lighthouses rising from the edge of rocky

The Rule of 86

Have you ever wondered how much maple sap it takes to make a gallon of syrup? As with many questions, this problem has been reduced to a mathematical formula, called Jones's Rule of 86. This rule states that if the collected maple sap contains 1 percent sugar, then it takes eighty-six gallons of sap to make one gallon of syrup. The average sugar maple tree produces sap with a sugar content of 2.2 percent. Using the Rule of 86, this means, on average, that it takes forty gallons of sap to make one gallon of syrup. Sap from red maples is much less sweet, with about eighty-six gallons required to make one gallon of syrup.

peninsulas are accented by autumn's brightest colors. Brightly painted lobster-trap buoys bob in the blue ocean amidst the scarlet reflections of maples growing along the shore. Blueberry barrens on sun-drenched hills are ablaze with an unbroken cloak of crimson.

Mount Desert Island is far enough north that the maples and oaks share the forest with evergreen spruce, pine, and juniper, making the fall foliage a mix of bright colors and cool green. The foliage season at Mount Desert Island peaks from late September to mid-October.

The Camden Hills are rugged and worn knobs of quartzite that loom over the working harbors of

Silver Cascade, New Hampshire

picturesque Penobscot Bay. The deciduous forests that cover the hills are magnificent in fall, the colors spilling down the mountains and reflecting off the shimmering ocean. West of Camden Hills State Park, framed by winding country roads, are the blueberry barrens. Peak foliage season in the Camden area is early to mid-October.

Pemaquid Peninsula is the place for the perfect postcard images of Maine. This picturesque yet rustic area has forests, harbor towns, lobster, and Pemaquid Point Light, one of the most famous lighthouses in the country. Foliage season on Pemaquid is about mid-October.

DRIVING TOURS

Acadia National Park: Mount Desert Island's 27-mile **Park Loop Road** (toll) circles a swarm of mountains that rise above the island's east shore. The western side of the loop is one-way (heading south), whereas the eastern side permits two-way traffic. The loop passes rough, beautiful landscapes scoured by wind-driven fog and bright sun. Autumn colors on Mount Desert Island are mostly red, burgundy, and juniper green. The auto road to the top of Cadillac Mountain (1,530 feet) begins near the north end of Park Loop Road.

Wiscasset to Waldoboro: Wiscasset, just northeast of Brunswick, is called the "prettiest village in Maine." The town is perched on the high shore above the wide Sheepscot River. From Wiscasset head north on Route 1, and enjoy the view while crossing the bridge over the Sheepscot River. At the beautiful harbor town of Newcastle, leave Route 1, and head south on combined Routes 129/130, which follow the Damariscotta River. At Prentiss Island follow Route 130 south along the Pemaquid peninsula. Continue on Route 130 south all the way to the beautiful views at Pemaquid Point, which include the famous Pemaquid Point Lighthouse. From

Pemaquid Point backtrack to Route 32, and follow Route 32 north the short distance to New Harbor, a fishing village with great lobster. Continue on Route 32 north past the Rachel Carson tidal pool, where the starfish are as colorful as the autumn leaves. The road follows Muscongus Sound back to Route 1 in Waldoboro. *Note:* Route 1 gets very busy during the fall foliage season.

Waldoboro to Bar Harbor and Mount Desert Island: From Waldoboro follow Route 1 north through Thomaston, Rockland, and north to Camden. Visit Camden harbor before continuing north past Camden Hills State Park and passing through many small towns lining Penobscot Bay. Follow Route 1 through Belfast to the northern end of the bay. Route 1 now crosses the Penobscot River and heads east past a number of lakes to Ellsworth. From the town of Ellsworth, follow Route 3 south, and cross the Mount Desert Narrows to Mount Desert Island. The road follows the north shore of the island before heading south to Bar Harbor.

HIKES WITH A VIEW

The Camden Hills: Ospreys fly over downtown Camden, and you can sit on a park bench and watch the windjammers slip in and out with the tide. But do journey to one of the most spectacular views in all of Maine, just a few minutes away: Camden Hills State Park. Mount Battie's worn quartzite summit holds a spectacular view that sweeps over the colorful wooded coastland and Camden harbor and across Penobscot Bay. **The Mount Battie Trail** leaves from Route 52 about 2 miles outside of Camden and affords a steep hike to the summit. For those not able to hike, there's a road you can drive to the top. Mount Battie's rocky summit is home to oaks and juniper, as well as to a stone viewing tower.

Beech leaves

Mount Megunticook is a long wooded ridge that traverses terrain called the tablelands, an open landscape with grass and shrubs. The views here are long and plentiful. **The Megunticook Ridge Trail** begins in the park's campground off of Route 1. The path wastes no time in beginning the fairly steep ascent of the ridge. At 1 mile the Ocean Lookout is reached, with views over Penobscot Bay and Mount Battie. The 2-mile round-trip hike is moderate to strenuous.

Acadia National Park: Bar Harbor Shore Path is an easy 1.5-mile round-trip walk along the shore of Bar Harbor on the east end of Mount Desert Island. The walk offers tranquil views of the harbor and islands. The trailhead is at the town pier in Bar Harbor.

If you're in good shape, you've got to climb Cadillac, the highest point in the park. The **Cadillac North Ridge Trail** begins at the North Ridge Cadillac parking area on an approximately 7-mile round-trip hike. The path is largely open with beautiful views over Bar Harbor far below.

Northeast

The Northeast boasts extensive tracts of unbroken forest, ancient mountains of folded bedrock, the shaded and serene streams of the Hudson Valley, and the craggy peaks and brilliant shimmering lakes of the Adirondacks of New York. The winding rugged terrain of the Delaware Water Gap in eastern Pennsylvania complements the vast wilderness of the Allegheny National Forest to the west. This region rivals New England for quality of fall color but adds the appealing option of more wide-open spaces, such as the 2.6 million acres of the Adirondack State Park in New York.

New York

New York's best fall foliage can be found in the Adirondacks, the Catskills, the Champlain Valley, the lower Hudson Valley, and the Finger Lakes. New York is steeped in history and tradition that make enjoying the sparkling fall foliage and magnificent countryside all the more delightful. Much of the state hosts mixed hardwood forests of maple, oak, ash, beech, and birch, with many less-abundant trees and shrubs completing the plant community. The evergreens pine, hemlock, arborvitae, spruce, and fir are common as well, especially in the North Country.

The foliage season in New York begins in the Adirondacks in early to mid-September and peaks there from mid-September to early October. The forests from the Champlain Valley down the Appalachians to Pennsylvania, including most of the Catskills, turn in late September and peak in the first half of October. The lower Hudson Valley and a wide corridor to the west along the Great Lakes, including the Finger Lakes region, peak in mid- to late October.

The Adirondacks

The Adirondacks are the crown jewels of New York, with treasures like Mount Marcy, New York's highest peak at 5,344 feet. This ancient mountain range lies between Lake Champlain and Lake Ontario. Adirondack Park is the largest wilderness preserve in the United States outside Alaska.

In the southern Adirondacks, the forest is a mix of birch, maple, beech, and other trees. Farther north, more conifers, such as fir and spruce, add some green to the fall display. In the higher elevations, like the High Peaks region, the dwarf plants above tree line often offer unique scarlet displays many days ahead of the rest of the region.

The Many Uses of Trees

The trees that we love and admire so much in fall have traditionally been used for some rather interesting things when they are harvested and sent to the sawmills. These are documented in a report from the U.S. Forest Service. For instance, maple sugar comes from sugar maple trees. But maples are also used to make dance floors, bowling alleys, and bowling pins. Lately specialty baseball bats have joined the list of maple products. Paper birch trees are the origin of some toothpicks, tongue depressors, and ice-cream sticks. Most people know that hickory is used for charcoal and tool handles, but it is also used for making the rungs of ladders. Flowering dogwood seems too small a tree to be used to make things, but the hard wood is a traditional source for pulleys and golf club heads. The wood from ash trees is used for many things, especially baseball bats. The white wood of tulip tree is used to make gunstocks as well as musical instruments. Hophornbeam is very hard, making it perfect for tool handles, mallets, and wooden canes. Sourwood trees were traditionally used to make the runners of sleds, tool handles, and machine bearings. The soft wood of aspen trees supplies us with matchsticks and paper pulp for newspaper. The durability of oak is important in the manufacture of mining timbers, caskets, barrels, kegs, and ships. If you want to make a small boat, sassafras is the traditional wood to use; it's good for fence posts too. Yellowwood was once used for gunstocks, and elm is the wood used for cheese boxes and hockey sticks. We admire the beauty of living trees, yet knowing what these magnificent plants become under our hand also allows the observer to build an appreciation for the unique traits and qualities of each species.

DRIVING TOUR

The Adirondack Trail: At exit 27 on I–90, head north on Route 30 to Riceville and Great Sacandaga Lake. Enter Adirondack Park, and follow the shore of the lake to Northville. Continue along the Sacandaga River to the junction with Route 8. Follow combined Routes 30/8 to Lake Pleasant, then continue north on Route 30 along the western shore of Indian Lake. At the junction of Route 28, follow combined Routes 28/30 to Blue Mountain Lake and the acclaimed Adirondack Museum. Continue north on Route 30 to Tupper Lake and Route 3. Follow combined Routes 3/30 a short distance east, then stay on Route 3 to the town of Saranac Lake. From here take Route 86 to Lake Placid.

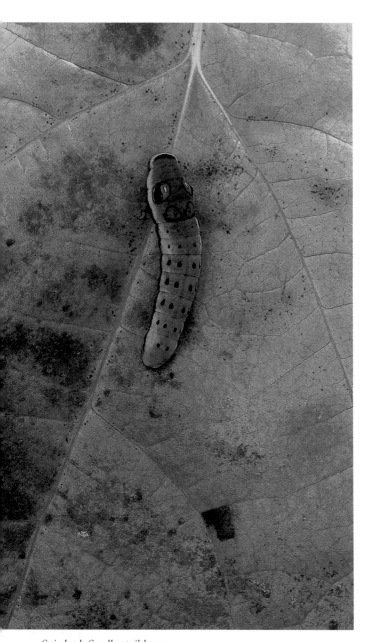

Spicebush Swallowtail larva

The Champlain Valley

Lake Champlain runs from southern Canada 125 miles down the New York and Vermont border. The first European to see the lake was Samuel de Champlain in 1609. From the French and Indian Wars through the War of 1812, the lake was the scene of many battles and was of strategic importance to the security of the northern frontier. Lake Champlain is also the alleged home of "Champ," the area's benign lake monster, who occasionally provides visitors with photo opportunities.

DRIVING TOUR

The Champlain Trail: From exit 21 on I–87 north of Glens Falls, take Route 9N north as it runs along the shore of beautiful Lake George over the Tongue Mountains to the town of Ticonderoga. Nearby, a short distance down Route 22, is Mount Defiance, a rocky promontory high above the narrows of Lake Champlain. From Ticonderoga continue north on combined Routes 9N/22 as they trace a path along the shore of Lake Champlain. At Westport follow Route 22 north to Plattsburgh.

HIKES WITH A VIEW

Buck Mountain rises above the east shore of Lake George and offers breathtaking views of the Green Mountains of Vermont to the east, the High Peaks of the Adirondacks to the west, and an ocean of fall foliage in between. The shimmering blue waters of Lake George lie 2,000 feet below. The hike is moderate and covers about 6 miles round-trip.

Lower Hudson Valley

This region of farm fields and pastures gave birth to the story of Rip van Winkle and Sleepy Hollow. The foliage display ranges from tracts of vibrant forest to the yellows and reds of hardwoods along hay fields and growing over rolling hills. The area is framed by the Catskills to the west and the Taconics to the east, with the broad Hudson River flowing through the heart of this charming valley.

DRIVING TOUR

The **Harlem Valley** is the name for the region west of the Taconic Mountains and east of the Hudson River in downstate southeast New York. At the junction of the Taconic State Parkway and Route 44 near Poughkeepsie, take the Taconic State Parkway north to Route 23. Follow Route 23 east to Route 22 in Hillsdale. Turn onto Route 22 south, and follow it along the foot of the Taconic Mountains past Taconic State Park, which has excellent hiking trails into the mountains. Continue to the junction with Route 44, and follow Route 44 back to Taconic State Parkway.

Catskill Mountains

Most of the Catskill Mountains are within Catskill Park, a 300,000-acre preserve in southeastern New York. The tallest—4,190-foot Slide Mountain—is near the center of the park. The mountains contain vast tracts of mixed hardwood forest that are brilliant in fall, as well as plentiful fields, waterfalls, and wildlife.

DRIVING TOUR

The Catskills: Begin at exit 90 on Route 17, a few miles east of the Pennsylvania border. Follow Route 30 along the East Branch of the Beaverkill River to Downsville

The Great Bear

Many Native American Nations that lived in the Northeast shared variations of a story that explained why the leaves turned shades of red each fall. The story is of a great malevolent bear with supernatural powers that is hunted by brothers who are regarded as the best hunters in all the land. The hunters chase the great bear through the forest and into the sky, where the brothers kill the bear. The blood from the bear falls from the sky and stains all the leaves red on the trees below. Hungry from the hunt, the brothers cook the bear. The hot fat from the meat drips from the sky and falls as snow, covering the land through winter.

Each year the hunt is played again in the sky. The great bear is the bowl of the constellation called the Big Dipper, also known as the Great Bear. The brothers are the stars of the dipper's handle. As the constellation moves across the sky, the bowl is upright until fall, when it turns upside down, spilling the blood of the bear onto the land. In spring it turns upright again, and the hunters and the bear resume their chase across the heavens.

and the intersection of Route 206. Continue on Route 30 along the shore of the Pepacton Reservoir to Margaretville and Route 28. Follow Route 28 as it now begins to travel deep into the Catskills, passing Big Indian, Phoenicia, and Mount Tremper before coming to the Ashokan Reservoir. At the Route 209 junction, follow Route 209 along the Roundout Creek back to Route 17 at exit 113.

HIKE WITH A VIEW

Balsam Lake Mountain Wild Forest: Alder Lake Loop Trail, an easy 1.5-mile loop trail (blazed red), follows the shore of Alder Lake. As with other lake loop trails, this walk has many beautiful spots that combine water and colorful woods. Alder Lake Trailhead is at the end of Alder Creek Road (County Route 54) in the town of Hardenburgh, Ulster County, 18 miles north of Livingston Manor (2.6 miles north of Turnwood).

Finger Lakes

The Finger Lakes in western New York are tucked between Lake Ontario to the north and Pennsylvania to the south. The beauty of the scenery here is unique, with the long, narrow lakes nestled in the rocky sinuous folds of the rolling hills.

Finger Lakes National Forest, New York's only national forest, is located in Hector, between Cayuga and Seneca Lakes southwest of Syracuse. It is tough to get lost here, as roads methodically divide the forest into square-mile blocks in the fashion of western counties. The terrain is a pleasing mix of open fields and forest, with more than 30 miles of hiking trails, the Interloken Trail being especially attractive. Wildlife is plentiful, and excellent viewing of deer, turkey, and raptors can often be done from the car.

Finger Lakes: From the Finger Lakes National Forest in Hector, travel north on Route 414. The east shore of the lake is prime winemaking country, and about seventeen vineyards dot the hills from Watkins Glen to Ovid. At the junction of Route 20, head east to Route 89 near the northern tip of Cayuga Lake, then follow Route 89 as it parallels the lakeshore all the way to the southern tip in Ithaca. In Ithaca take Route 79 west toward Seneca Lake. Turn southwest onto Route 227, and follow it to the intersection with Route 414 at the southern tip of Seneca Lake. Turn north onto Route 414, and return to Hector and the Finger Lakes National Forest.

Pennsylvania and New Jersey

From the New Jersey Skylands in the east to the Laurel Mountains in the west, this area encompasses hundreds of miles of mountains, rivers, ravines, waterfalls, and far-reaching overlooks. The trees that paint this landscape in fall include hickory, oak, maple, birch, beech, and ash. Sassafras, aspen, and willow can be found along wide river valleys, whereas evergreen hemlock likes the cool rocky ravines near streams and cascades. Beneath the forest canopy are redbud, witch-hazel, and juneberry.

The foliage season begins to peak first in the high country in early October and extends to mid- to late October. Most of the region usually peaks in mid-October through late October. The area around Hawk Mountain in southeast Pennsylvania often peaks in late October and can extend into early November.

Northwest New Jersey

The focus of the **New Jersey Skylands** is the Delaware Water Gap National Recreation Area, which runs from

Deer skull and autumn leaves

I–80 in the south to nearly the New York border in the north. The centerpiece of the Gap is the Delaware River, which casually snakes through the valley with a relaxed genuine beauty. The river is guided in its meanders by imposing rocky ridges with views from the top that definitely get the adrenaline pumping.

DRIVING TOUR

Delaware Water Gap: Get the maps out, as this tour travels through back roads along the edge of the Gap to Milford, Pennsylvania. From exit 1 off I–80, head northeast on River Road. The road runs close to the river and passes a number of islands. The steep slopes of Kittatinny Mountain are on the right. A number of roads wind through the Gap, some keeping close to the river, others climbing to the ridge. Continue northwest toward Millbrook, then Flatbrookville. An attractive road passes along Flat Brook going by Tillman Ravine Natural Area and Flat Brook and Roy State Wildlife Management Areas. At the junction of Route 521, follow it north through Hainsville State Wildlife Management Area to Milford.

HIKE WITH A VIEW

High Point State Park: Near the northern end of the Delaware Water Gap is High Point State Park, with great views of the fall foliage from the highest point in New Jersey. The park is just north of Sussex on Route 23, where New Jersey meets Pennsylvania and New York. The 14,000-acre preserve has a visitor center, camping, and Lake Marcia, a spring-fed pond ringed with colorful hardwoods. The Monument Trail (3.5 miles long) passes through the highest-elevation Atlantic white cedar swamp in the world, then visits the nature center and a 220-foot monument at the crest of the hill. Along the

way there are sweeping views of mountains and valleys cloaked in fall's splendor.

Eastern Pennsylvania

HIKES WITH A VIEW

Hawk Mountain Sanctuary: The view from Hawk Mountain in Kempton extends for 70 miles over the beautiful valleys and ridges of the Blue Mountains. But it's at its best when dressed in all the colors of fall. The North Lookout is particularly inspiring. Hawk Mountain is one of the world's best places to watch the spectacular annual migration of raptors. The 8-mile network of trails includes overlooks where nearly 20,000 hawks, falcons, and eagles soar past the cliffs each fall on their way south.

Western Pennsylvania

DRIVING TOUR

Laurel Highlands Scenic Byway runs about 70 miles from Seward to Farmington near the West Virginia border. The journey is truly relaxing and scenic, with miles and miles of pastoral countryside. Farms and attractive small towns mix with green pastures and vibrant fall foliage. From Seward travel southwest on Route 711 to I–76 in Donegal. Continue southwest on the Laurel Highlands Scenic Byway as it becomes Route 381. Falling Water, Frank Lloyd Wright's most famous house, is near Mill Run. Ohiopyle State Park is another beautiful stop before the byway ends near Farmington.

HIKE WITH A VIEW

Youghiogheny River Trail: When trains no longer run on a section of track, the path is frequently reborn as a

Scarlet oak

rail trail. The Youghiogheny River Trail in the Laurel Highlands is such a creation, with a graded bed for easy walking and marvelous views of the striking foliage. The portion of trail in Ohiopyle State Park parallels the Youghiogheny River and provides easy walking to stunning natural features ablaze with brightly colored leaves. The hard-surfaced trail is also open to bikes.

Midwest

Away from the Midwest's fertile fields, an entirely different countryside emerges: a region influenced and defined by the Great Lakes, drained by mammoth river systems and strewn with glacial ponds and hills. In fall the vast maple forests light up the landscape with fiery colors.

The foliage trail through the Midwest is a web of paths leading to surprisingly varied and splendid places. The climate and soils support a diverse array of deciduous trees that produce reliable color year after year.

Wisconsin

Wisconsin is where the cheese is as orange as the autumn leaves, and glossy red fall color is as likely to come from ripe cranberries as from sugar maple leaves. The vast forests of this state contain a wide variety of deciduous trees known for their expressive fall color. A walk or drive through the Wisconsin countryside is a spectacle of yellow, orange, and red leaves from elms, ash, maples, oaks, aspen, willow, and birch. The time of peak foliage in Wisconsin ranges from early October in the north to mid-October in the south.

DRIVING TOUR

The Cranberry Highway: The heart of Wisconsin holds a fall treasure unmatched in most of the country—the harvest of billions of luminescent red cranberries. This 50-mile trip runs through Wisconsin's cranberry country, including a drive along the Wisconsin River and Nepco Lake. At cranberry harvest time each marsh is flooded; the water is contained by grassy dikes that ring the boggy fields. Machines loosen the berries from the plants, and the buoyant cranberries bob on the surface. The scene is amazing, with countless shiny berries forming a scarlet mat across the marsh.

There are 15,000 acres of cranberry marshes in Wisconsin and nearly as many places along the Cranberry Highway to stop and sample the ingenious ways to prepare this native fruit. A visitor center is located in Wisconsin Rapids. The harvest season for cranberries, from the end of September to the end of October, coincides with the foliage season.

HIKES WITH A VIEW

The Ice Age Trail: Thousands of years ago a massive mile-high glacier slowly advanced over what is now the state of Wisconsin, bulldozing huge piles of rock and soil ahead of it. When the climate warmed and the ice retreated, traces of the extinct glacier remained in the sinuous mounds that marked the boundary of the glacier's furthest advance. These long mounds, called terminal moraines, form the course of a unique hiking path called the Ice Age Trail. The Ice Age Trail runs 1,200 miles in a horseshoe-shaped loop from Sturgeon Bay on Lake Huron to near St. Croix Falls on the Mississippi River and is divided into nine sections. Parts of the trail are still under construction.

The Ice Age Trail (portions are a National Scenic Trail) crosses glacial features like moraines, kettles, kames, eskers, and drumlins—and that is just a start. These features enhance the fall foliage that is so abundant on this trail.

A great place to explore the Ice Age Trail is the Kettle Moraine State Forest–Southern Unit in the southeast corner of Wisconsin. The 21,000-acre forest has abundant hardwood forests and great views.

Apostle Islands National Lakeshore: This is as far north as you can go in Wisconsin, and it is well worth the trip. The Apostle Islands consist of twenty-one islands in Lake Superior and 12 miles of lakeshore on the mainland. The 69,000-acre preserve boasts sea caves, cliffs, sandy beaches, old-growth forests, and six lighthouses. More than 50 miles of hiking trails snake over the islands, leading to abandoned quarries, old farms and logging camps, and overlooks with long views across Lake Superior. Wherever you go, the foliage is spectacular.

Tulip poplar leaf

Michigan

This large state is nearly completely surrounded by the long views and rolling waves of the Great Lakes. Massive sand dunes, long beaches, and brilliant lighthouses hug the shore. Inland are beautiful rivers and woodland lakes. In fall the extensive deep forests of hardwoods such as maple, oak, and beech ignite the woods with spectacular color.

DRIVING TOUR

Leelanau Peninsula: From Cadillac head west on Route 55, past Lake Mitchell and into the heart of Manistee National Forest. The deciduous trees in the Manistee Forest, like maples and aspens, blanket the woods with warm shades of red and gold. The peak time here is mid-October inland and a little later toward the lakeshore. From near the town of Manistee, take Route 22 along the shore of Lake Michigan and through the amazing landscape of Sleeping Bear Dunes. Here the sand dunes are hundreds of feet high, and the views over the lake are indescribable. Continue on Route 22 as it makes a circuit around the Leelanau Peninsula, finally heading south to Traverse City.

HIKE WITH A VIEW

Bald Mountain State Recreation Area: This exciting recreation area is more than 4,500 acres of beautifully diverse countryside. Forests of maple, oak, and beech turn to red, orange, and bronze from late September to early October. There are attractive fields, lakes, and streams to explore on 15 miles of trails, including deep green cedar swamps. Bald Mountain is located just north of Detroit off Route 24.

Michigan Chestnut Trees

At the beginning of the twentieth century, the American chestnut *(Castanea dentata)* made up more than one-quarter of all the trees in the forests of the eastern states. The largest trees stood more than 100 feet tall, with trunks 4 feet in diameter. In fewer than fifty years, however, nearly all the chestnuts—numbering in the billions—were gone. The cause of this ecological massacre was the accidental introduction of the chestnut blight fungus, which benignly infects Asian chestnuts but is lethal to the American species. When infected Asian trees were brought to New York in 1904, the epidemic began. The fungus most often kills the above-ground portion of the tree, leaving the roots to resprout. In this manner the chestnut has survived as stump sprouts scattered through the woods for nearly a century.

Most of Michigan is outside the native range of the American chestnut, but generations ago some pioneers intrepidly planted groves of the trees near their homesteads. Many of these small stands were isolated enough to escape the blight. Some of these trees are dying as the blight eventually reaches them. But other infected trees are not dying. These trees have served for decades as a resource for researchers who are trying to breed resistance into the American chestnut. As you wander the roads and trails of Michigan, be on the lookout. The long-toothed chestnut leaves turn bronze and gold in fall, with brown chestnut burrs clinging to the twigs.

Ohio

The most spectacular forests for fall foliage can be found along the bluffs and hills near the Ohio River in southern Ohio. Here approximately eighty-seven different tree species grow within a plant community that blends northern trees, like sugar maple, with southern trees, such as blackjack oak. The region also has a number of trees that seem particularly adapted to areas like the Ohio Valley, including pawpaw, Ohio buckeye, and fringe tree. So many types of trees produces a fall color display that is colorful and diverse.

DRIVING TOUR

Wayne National Forest and Ohio River: From Marietta take Route 7 as it meanders between the Wayne National Forest and the bank of the Ohio River. The road passes the Willow Island Lock and Dam before reaching Newport. Continuing on Route 7, the Leith Run Recreation Area is reached near the trailhead for the Ohio View trail.

Follow Route 260 through the Wayne National Forest, passing the north trailhead for the Ohio View Trail midway to Bloomfield. In Bloomfield take Route 26 south as it weaves along the Little Muskingum River to the Rinard Covered Bridge. Just beyond the junction with Route 408 is the Hune Covered Bridge, then the Hills Covered Bridge as you near Marietta.

HIKE WITH A VIEW

Serpent Mound State Memorial: About 75 miles east of Cincinnati, in Peebles, is a serpentine earthen structure that weaves more than 1,000 feet through the dense hardwood forest. The undulating mound of earth depicts a giant snake with its tail coiled and jaws agape, forever frozen mid-strike. People of the Adena or Fort Ancient cultures may have built it up to 2,000 years ago, but no one knows for sure. The Serpent Mound is the largest such structure of its kind in the world. The huge snake sits on an attractive bluff above the Ohio Brush Creek.

On the grounds of Serpent Mound State Memorial is a 30-foot observation tower with the best views of the serpent beneath you. In fall the grassy body of the snake seems to slide beneath the yellow, orange, and red canopies of the trees. It's a great visual effect.

The South

The South is dotted with an amazingly varied and vibrant array of fall foliage destinations. Although the climate in much of the region is too warm to produce strong fall color, the southern mountains, from the Appalachians to the Ozarks, are a wonderful exception. Along the spine of this ancient range grow wonderfully diverse forests where species common in the North, such as sugar maple, scarlet oak, and black birch, mingle with southern trees like tupelo, sweet gum, and yellowwood. The numerous species in this rugged landscape produce myriad kaleidoscopic views. The intensity of color and breadth of coverage across the Appalachian landscape is close to that of New England. The cooler climate of the mountains produces a peak foliage season with similar start and end dates as locations farther north, from early to mid-October in the Great Smokies to late October and early November in the Appalachians of Georgia. In fall the scenic routes through the mountains from Virginia to Georgia are crowded with cars and trailers that make the going slow.

The Blue Ridge Mountains

Skyline Drive, which becomes the Blue Ridge Parkway, provides perhaps the most beautiful ride in America, snaking through the mountains of Virginia and North Carolina. During the foliage season, when vibrant fall colors paint the mountains, gorges, waterfalls, and vistas, this route comes close to a paradise.

The forests of the Virginia and North Carolina mountains contain a vibrant mix of northern and southern species. Foliage season runs from late September through October, with the earliest color appearing high up the mountains.

The Blue Ridge Mountains are part of the Appalachians, which run from New England to Georgia. Skyline Drive and the Blue Ridge Parkway span 469 miles between Shenandoah National Park and the Great Smoky Mountains, with numerous campgrounds, historic sites, overlooks, and hiking trails.

DRIVING TOUR

The Blue Ridge Parkway is a scenic tourist road for leisurely travel. This applies throughout the year but more so during foliage season.

From the northern terminus of Skyline Drive in Virginia, just west of Washington D.C., head south from Front Royal. The first 217 miles wind through Virginia and the Shenandoah Mountains, and the final 252 miles cross North Carolina to the Great Smoky Mountains east of the Tennessee border. The following visitor centers offer good foliage views.

Visitor Center	Mile #
Humpback Rocks	5.8
James River Overlook	63.6
Peaks of Otter	85.6
Rocky Knob	167.1
Cumberland Knob	217.5
Moses Cove Memorial Park	293.5
Linn Cove Viaduct	304.4
Linnville Falls	316.4
Museum of Minerals	330.9
Craggy Gardens	364.4
Folk Art Center	380.1
Mount Pisgah	408.6
Waterrock Knob	451.0

HIKES WITH A VIEW

Virginia

- Sharp Top Trail (mile 86). Strenuous 1.6-mile hike leaving from the store, climbing steeply to the crest of Sharp Top Mountain and a 360-degree view.
- Appalachian Trail (mile 95.9). A moderate 1-mile hike from Montevale overlook to Taylor's Mountain overlook.

North Carolina

- Cedar Ridge Trail (mile 238.5). A 4.2-mile moderate hike through beautiful forest and views.
- Flat Rock Trail (mile 308.6). An easy half-mile walk to a view of Grandfather Mountain, one of the most spectacular mountains in the East.
- Linnville Falls Trail (mile 316.4). A moderate walk through old-growth forest to a stunning waterfall.

Hornbeam leaves

- Lost Cove Ridge Trail (mile 350.4). A moderate hike of about 3.3 miles to a lookout tower with a grand 360-degree view.
- Mount Pisgah Trail (mile 407.6). Strenuous 1.3-mile hike to summit of Mount Pisgah (5,721 feet) and a 360-degree view.
- Waterrock Knob Trail (mile 451.2). A 1.2-mile hike to a mountain crest and beautiful views.

The Great Smokies

Incredible natural beauty and a wide array of interesting history combine to make the Smokies a fascinating place. There are hiking trails, beautiful streams, and dozens of historic places to visit. Fall foliage peaks in the Smokies about mid-October.

DRIVING TOUR

Great Smoky Mountains: Newfound Gap Road bisects Great Smoky Mountain National Park and offers a slice of the many varied sights in these beautiful mountains. The road covers a bit more than 30 miles, but because of its popularity, it will probably take you hours to complete. Midweek is a little less congested, but if you wait until a few days after peak, the roadways are more open.

The Newfound Gap Road begins at the Sugarlands Visitor Center near Gatlinburg, Tennessee. A few miles past the visitor center are paths that venture off into the sugar bush. The woods here are full of the sugar maples that give the Sugarland Valley its name and that make this area particularly beautiful at this time of year. A few miles down the road is the Campbell Overlook, which offers a stunning view of Mount LeConte (6,593 feet).

The road continues to climb toward the divide along the Tennessee and North Carolina border. Near the one-third mark is the Alum Cave Bluff Parking Area. The Alum Cave Bluff Trail provides a strenuous 2.3-

Why Are the Smokies Smoky?

A really clear day can be hard to come by in the Great Smoky Mountains and the nearby Blue Ridge Mountains. While other mountain ranges are clear, a persistent bluish haze hangs over the valleys and obscures the distant hills in a soft smoky fog that gives these mountains their descriptive names. The hazy skies have been here for centuries, long before the industrial revolution. But it is only recently that some of the answers regarding this mysterious haze have been partially understood.

As plants grow they produce many chemicals, including many organic hydrocarbons, such as ethylene, isoprene, and terpenes. Apples give off ethylene, oaks emit isoprene, and conifers produce terpenes. As terpenes are released into the air, they react with sunlight and ozone and change from a vapor into extremely tiny particles that are suspended in the air. The particles are just the right size to reflect blue light when sunlight strikes them, producing the bluish smoky haze you see on the horizon. Terpene emissions are greatest on warm days, in the spring, and at lower elevations.

mile (one-way) hike to Alum Cave Bluff. At 13 miles is the beautiful Morton Overlook, followed by Newfound Gap, where Tennessee and North Carolina meet. It's also where the Appalachian Trail crosses the road on its way from Georgia to Maine.

Past the gap are a series of overlooks in the next few miles. One of the most beautiful is Oconoluftee, with views down the Oconoluftee Valley. From this overlook to the end of the road at the Oconoluftee visitor center are numerous stops that celebrate local history.

HIKE WITH A VIEW

Clingman's Dome: Just beyond Newfound Gap on Newfound Gap Road is Clingman's Dome Road. Follow the road 7.5 miles to the Clingman's Dome parking area. From here it is a 0.5-mile hike on an easy trail to the summit (the Appalachian Trail crosses the mountain here) and an observation tower. The view here is spectacular, with long vistas down the valleys and great views of nearby mountains, including Mount Mitchell (6,684 feet), the highest mountain east of the Mississippi. Clingman's Dome, at 6,642 feet, is the highest point in the park and on the entire Appalachian Trail.

Georgia

Like migrating songbirds, the bright colors of autumn head south too—all the way to Georgia. The northwest part of the state hosts the southern edge of the Appalachian Mountains. Peak season is late October into November. Trees to look for include crimson-red sourwood, yellow hickories, and scarlet maples.

DRIVING TOUR

The **Chattahoochee National Forest** is on the border of Tennessee and North and South Carolina. From Helen, within the Brasstown Ranger District, travel north on Routes 17/75 through the woodlands of the Chattahoochee National Forest. Color peaks here at the end of October through early November. Take Route 180 west to Georgia Spur 180 on the right. Follow the spur to the visitor center at Brasstown Bald. Brasstown Bald, at more than 4,700 feet, is the highest point in Georgia and overlooks rounded wooded hills drenched in color. The observation deck offers views into four states. From Brasstown Bald continue west to combined Route 19/129. Turn north toward Blairesville, passing through very pretty countryside to Route 76. Turn onto Route 76 east, passing Chatuge Lake and Hiawassee, to Route 17/75. Turn south onto Route 17/75, and enjoy the trip back to Helen.

HIKE WITH A VIEW

Slaughter Creek Trail: Slaughter Creek was named for an ancient battle between the Creek and Cherokee Indians. The trail runs 2.7 miles from the Lake Winfield Scott Recreation Area on Route 180 to the Appalachian Trail (AT) at Slaughter Gap. The walk is moderate, with abundant hardwood forest above thickets of mountain laurel and rhododendron. Views along the way are beautiful. From the AT junction at Slaughter Gap near Slaughter Creek, it is about a 1-mile walk along the AT to Blood Mountain with more fine views.

Arkansas

Arkansas has some of the best fall foliage anywhere. The Ozark forests have a wonderful variety of trees, including sassafras, maples, poplars, oaks, sumac, and sweet gum. The foliage—combined with countryside replete with bluffs and overlooks, interesting rock formations, and winding valleys—makes visiting here a treat. Peak foliage season is the first two weeks of November.

Ozark Mountains: This trip has some great color and tours the rolling hills of Quachita National Forest. From Hot Springs follow Route 7 north to Ola. In Ola head south on Route 27 to Mount Ida, then back to Hot Springs on Route 270.

HIKE WITH A VIEW

King's Bluff Loop Trail: This 2-mile moderate loop trail is a stunning walk that passes through lots of deep hardwood forest smoldering with color. In parts the path traces a line along the edge of tall cliffs to King's Bluff, where inspiring views of the vivid countryside spill out below. Don't miss the waterfall that drops over the sandstone ridge. The trailhead is about 6 miles east of Pelsor on Route 16.

Rocky Mountains

The Rocky Mountains are a region of high valleys and windswept plateaus surrounded by saw-toothed peaks and ranges. The best foliage is found in the sheltered hollows of canyons, down the keels of mountain valleys, and on the lee slopes of ridges. In the fall aspens rule the Rockies with larch, alder, willow, and huckleberry providing wonderful secondary colors. Together the trees glow with shades of sunset peach or radiate a pure yellow so intense it is reminiscent of the sun at dawn diffusing through a bank of fog.

The peak foliage season in the Rockies generally occurs during late September in the high mountain valleys to mid-October.

Colorado

DRIVING TOUR

San Juan Mountains: From Durango head north on Route 550 into San Juan National Forest. Look for areas of bright color along the Animas River and Electra Lake. Continue through Red Mountain Pass (11,000 feet). At the town of Ridgway, turn onto Route 62, passing through Dallas Divide (8,970 feet). At Placerville turn south onto Route 145, and follow the flow of the San Miguel River toward Telluride. Continue south through Lizard Head Pass (10,222 feet) before descending to the Dolores River Valley. From here to the town of Dolores there are great areas of color. At the junction of Routes 145 and 184, turn east onto 184, and follow that to Route 160. Continue east on Route 160 back to Durango.

HIKES WITH A VIEW

The Colorado Trail extends some 500 miles from just south of Denver to Durango. Along the way the trail passes through seven national forests and over eight mountain ranges. The views are exceptional. A much more sedate walk can be enjoyed along the **Animas River Trail** in Durango, which follows the river as it flows through town.

Utah and Idaho

DRIVING TOUR

Wasatch Mountains and Bear Lake: From Ogden take Route 39 (Canyon Road) east into the Wasatch-Cache National Forest. The road traces the canyons of the Ogden River, where the fall foliage is spectacular. In Woodruff follow Route 16 north along the Bear River Valley through Randolf, then take Route 30 toward

Aspens

Bear Lake. At Garden City continue north along the lake on Route 89, following it through Paris to the junction of Route 36. Travel west on Route 36 through Caribou National Forest to Preston, an area with reliable fall color. From Preston follow Route 91 south to Logan.

HIKE WITH A VIEW

Wasatch Mountains: Hidden Valley Trail begins in the city of Ogden on the Indian Trail off Twenty-second Street. The path climbs into the Wasatch Mountains through attractive country wooded with aspen that is beautiful in fall. The round-trip (about 4 miles) is strenuous, but the views over Ogden are very satisfying.

Wyoming and Montana

DRIVING TOUR

Yellowstone Park and Gallatin National Forest: From Jackson head north on Route 26/89 into the breathtaking scenery of the awesome Grand Teton Mountains. Continue north through the Snake River Valley to Route 287. Follow Route 287 (toll) along the northeast shore of Jackson Lake, then along the Lewis River valley to the south entrance of Yellowstone Park. From the south entrance continue north past Lewis Lake to West Thumb on the shore of Yellowstone Lake, where the road forks.

The west loop follows the Firehole and Gibbons Rivers past Old Faithful geyser to Madison. From Madison the road jogs east and north to Norris and the Norris–Canyon Road, which, aptly enough, connects Norris and Canyon. Continue north from Norris to Mammoth Hot Springs.

The east loop traces a path around the northwest shore of beautiful Yellowstone Lake, then follows the Yellowstone River toward Canyon. From Canyon the road heads north to Tower Falls before swinging west to Mammoth Hot Springs.

From Mammoth Hot Springs head north on Route 89, entering Montana and leaving Yellowstone Park via the north entrance. The highway continues along the Yellowstone Valley through Gardiner and into the Gallatin National Forest. Continue north on Route 89 to I–90, and take the interstate west into Bozeman.

HIKES WITH A VIEW

Yellowstone: The conditions of trails in Yellowstone can change quickly, and trails can be closed because of weather, high water levels, forest fires, and bear activity. Visit a national ranger station or visitor center for current information.

For those in good shape, the 11-mile trek to **Observation Peak** begins at the Cascade Lake Picnic Area 1.5 miles north of Canyon Junction on the Tower–Canyon Road. The trail leads to Cascade Lake, then up a steep slope to the summit, which holds amazing views of Yellowstone far below. This hike is strenuous.

Fall Foliage in Unexpected Places

Pockets of autumn splendor are scattered unexpectedly across the country from the Atlantic to the Pacific and from near Canada to Mexico. Like bright seashells that glimmer against a monotone of sand, these destinations provide an unanticipated bounty to the seeker of fall's grandeur.

Texas

Ranch Road 187 passes through miles and miles of flat dry Texas plains dotted with scrub and cacti. It is very easy to believe that there isn't a living maple tree within a thousand miles. But they are here, and in abundance.

Red maple leaves, mushrooms on a birch log

Lost Maples Natural Area, outside San Antonio, is a network of canyons carved from the limestone bedrock by the rivers and streams that drain the countryside. The sheltered hollows provide a moist, cool microclimate that protects the area from the more arid and hotter climate of the plateau. The preserve encompasses more than 2,000 acres and is a sanctuary for many species of birds and animals as well as a population of canyon maples *(Acer grandidentatum)*.

Canyon maples are also called bigtooth maples for the prominent lobes on the leaf. The foliage is exceptional for this part of the country and turns from medium green to shades of pink, orange, and red, with occasional trees showing the brilliant tones familiar in more northerly climes. The best color is seen on trees growing right along the creeks and rivers, as well as in thickets on the canyon and valley walls. Peak foliage occurs from the last few days of October to the third week of November.

DRIVING TOUR

At Lost Maples the driving tour is short and sweet. The paved access road into Lost Maples runs for about a mile along the Sabinal River past a picnic area and campground. The road is restful in its scenery, with shady woods, and the unhurried flow of the Sabinal River adds to the relaxed atmosphere. Lost Maples can get crowded during foliage season, especially during the weekends.

HIKE WITH A VIEW

Lost Maples was designed for hikers, with about 10 miles of trails. The easiest path is Maple Trail, a short and level (0.4 mile) interpretive trail along the Sabinal River. East Trail (4.5 miles) loops through the Can Creek valley past small lakes and rugged bedrock cliffs with great views into the forested canyon.

Washington and Oregon

The irresistible object (the Cascade Range) meets the unstoppable force (the Columbia River): The result is the majestic Columbia River Gorge, about 80 miles long and 4,000 feet deep. Vine maples, aspens, cottonwoods, Oregon ash, and big leaf maples brighten the landscape with infinite shades of yellows and reds, and huckleberries ignite clearings with ember red leaves. Peak foliage season in the gorge usually runs from the last week in October to the first week of November.

DRIVING TOUR

Route 14 through the Columbia River Gorge: Begin in Skamania, and drive east past the Bonneville Dam through North Bonneville and on to Stevenson. Good pockets of fall foliage can usually be seen between Stevenson and Bingen. The best place to find bright colors, however, is along the stretch from Bingen to Lyle.

HIKES WITH A VIEW

Columbia Gorge Trails: The Dog Mountain Trail begins 13 miles east of Stevenson on Route 14. The path is 3.1 miles long (one way) and steeply climbs to sweeping views of the Cascades with Mount St. Helens, Mount Hood, and Mount Adams in the distance. This strenuous trail can be crowded.

The Pacific Crest Trail is the long-distance trail of the West Coast, running 2,600 miles from Mexico to Canada. To hike a portion of this famous trail, take Route 14 to the information booth at the north end of Bridge of the Gods toll road. The trailhead is 90 yards down the road. Sights that are fairly close include the Cedar and Hamilton Canyons.

The Saint Cloud Day Use Site Trail is very short (0.5 mile round-trip) and easy, taking you to the largest

Frost on red maple leaf

remaining natural wetland in the gorge. The vista is open and sunny, with dense thickets of Himalayan blueberry. The trailhead is 0.1 mile west of milepost 30 on Route 14 in Skamania.

Arizona

The Mongollon Escarpment, a sheer rock wall as much as 2,000 feet high, runs diagonally across much of northeast Arizona. The Mongollon Rim is the very edge of the escarpment and is rich in natural and historic wonders, including canyons, lakes, and most surprisingly, fall foliage. The best place to view the foliage is in the canyons and near lakes where aspen, willow, and oaks provide color. Peak season along the rim runs from late October to early November.

DRIVING TOUR

Rim Road: Scenic features on this trip include the Mongollon Rim, Barbershop Canyon, East Clear Creek, and the General Crook Trail. From Clints Well and Happy Jacks, about 50 miles south of Flagstaff, drive north on Forest Road (FR) 87 to the junction with FR 95. Head generally south, following in succession FR 95 to FR 96, FR 96 to FR 321, and FR 321 to FR 300. Drive along FR 300, which traces the rim to Arizona Route 87. Turn north onto Arizona Route 87, and return to the starting point.

HIKE WITH A VIEW

The Arizona Trail: This moderate trail runs about 8 miles from near Blue Ridge Reservoir to the General Springs Cabin and the junction with the General Crook Trail. Fall foliage is especially evident in the canyons along the way. From the reservoir the path crosses the East Clear Creek and wanders into East Clear Creek Canyon. As it leaves the canyon, the trail crosses terrain that offers beautiful long views as the path climbs to Battleground Ridge. From here the path winds its way through General Springs Canyon to its intersection with the General Crook Trail and the General Springs Cabin.

Resources

Foliage Hotlines and Web Sites

Tauk Foliage Hotline, (800) 214–8209

Yankee Magazine,
www.yankeefoliage.com

This colorful site is easy to navigate and has lots of useful information, especially about New England. Has foliage maps, updated peak foliage destination information, weather forecasts for the region, trips, and driving tours.

USDA Forest Service, (800) 354–4595, ww.fs.fed.us/news/fallcolors

A great place to start your search for places to visit, the USDA Forest Service Web site contains information on national forests across the country, with hot spots and links. Also has direct links to a number of state foliage sites, as well as many very good private sites.

In addition, many states offer specific information tailored to visitors. This can be found by using these phone numbers or Web sites. Most will send travel guides with maps and/or provide information on lodging and special events.

New England

Connecticut
Connecticut Vacation Center, (800) 282–6863, www.ctbound.org

Maine
Maine Office of Tourism, (800) 533–9595, www.visitmaine.com

Massachusetts
Massachusetts Department of Tourism, (800) 227–6277, www.massvacation.com

New Hampshire
New Hampshire Tourism, (800) 258–3608, www.visitnh.gov

Rhode Island
Rhode Island Travel Center, (800) 556–2484, www.visitrhodeisland.com

Vermont
Vermont Travel Packets only, (800) 837–6668
Vermont Department of Tourism, (802) 828–3237, www.vermontvacation.com

Northeast/Mid-Atlantic

New York
New York State Travel Info Center, (800) 225–5697, www.iloveny.com

Delaware
Delaware Tourism, (800) 441–8846, www.visitdelaware.com

Maryland
Maryland hotline, (800) 532–8371

New Jersey
New Jersey Travel and Tourism, (800) 537–7397, www.visitnj.org

West Virginia
West Virginia Tourism, (800) 225–5982, www.callwva.com

Midwest/Great Plains

Indiana
Indiana Tourism Division, (800) 289–6646, www.enjoyindiana.com

Iowa
Iowa Fall Foliage Hotline, (515) 233–4110

Michigan
Michigan Travel Information, (800) 644–3255, www.michigan.org

Minnesota
Minnesota Office of Tourism, (800) 657–3700, www.exploreminnesota.com

Ohio
Ohio Travel Info Hotline, (800) 282–5393, www.ohiotourism.com

Oklahoma
Oklahoma Tourism, (800) 652–6552

Wisconsin
Wisconsin Tourism, (800) 372–2737, www.travelwisconsin.com

The South

Alabama
Alabama Tourism & Travel, (800) 252–2262, www.touralabama.org

Arkansas
Arkansas Tourism, (800) 628–8725, www.arkansas.com

Kentucky
Kentucky Department of Travel, (800) 225–8747, www.kentuckytourism.com

North Carolina
North Carolina Travel and Tourism, (800) 847–4862, www.visitnc.com

South Carolina
South Carolina Travel Information, (800) 849–4766, www.theupcountry.com

Tennessee
Tennessee Fall Color Forecast, (800) 697–4200, www.tandvacation.com

Texas
Texas Travel Information, (800) 452–9292, www.dot.state.tex.us

Georgia
Georgia Tourism, (800) 847–4842, www.georgiaonmymind.org

Virginia
Shenandoah Valley Foliage Hotline, (800) 434–5323
Shenandoah National Park, (540) 999–3500, www.nps.gov

West

Colorado
Colorado Tourism, (800) COLORADO, www.colorado.com

Idaho
Idaho Tourism, (800) 847–4843, www.visitid.org

Montana
Montana Tourism, (800) 847–4868, www.visitmt.com

Oregon
Oregon Tourism, (800) 547–5445, www.visitlanecounty.org

Utah
Utah Tourism Industry Coalition, (435) 425–3997, www.utahtourism.org

Wyoming
Wyoming Travel & Tourism, (800) 225–5996, www.wyomingtourism.org

About the Author

Charles W. G. Smith is an award-winning author and former Horticulture Editor at Storey Publishing. He has also served as Contributing Editor of *Fine Gardening* magazine and teaches horticulture courses for the Massachusetts College of Liberal Arts at the Berkshire Botanical Garden. His recent books include *The Weather-Resilient Garden* and *Raptor!: A Kid's Guide to Birds of Prey*. He has also written books on hiking and canoeing in New England. He's an avid outdoorsman living in Massachusetts with his wife Susan and their several children.

About the Photographer

Frank Kaczmarek is a professional biologist whose nature photographs have appeared in numerous magazines, calendars, and books. He currently resides in Oakdale, Connecticut.